STARTING TO COLLECT SERIES

# ANTIQUE ORIENTAL RUGS

# STARTING TO COLLECT SERIES

# ANTIQUE ORIENTAL RUGS

Murray Lee Eiland III

ANTIQUE COLLECTORS' CLUB

ISBN 1 85149 406 5

British Library Cataloguing-in-Publication Data
A catalogue record for this book is available from the British Library

Frontispiece: *Afshar rug, see Figure 62*

Published by the Antique Collectors' Club Ltd., Woodbridge, Suffolk, England
Printed and bound in Spain

# Contents

# ACKNOWLEDGEMENTS

Preparing a short work with such a wide scope is no easy task. Unlike a larger book, with more space to work out important issues, a short work needs rapidly to address important points before moving on. Images are therefore of primary interest, as these make up for the limited amount of space devoted to text.

Many organisations and private individuals have provided me with transparencies of excellent quality. Detlef Maltzahn of Rippon Boswell in Wiesbaden kindly supplied a wide range of examples, and has generously informed me about the state of the market in Germany. Taher Sabahi, in his capacity as editor of *Ghereh*, has also contributed, and has been a critical source of information for many years. Roger and Conroy Cavanna, of Carpets of the Inner Circle in San Francisco, have made available transparencies from their impressive collection of Persian city rugs, while Sandra Whitman has loaned transparencies of the Chinese rugs in which she has specialised. James Opie has contributed illustrations of south Persian rugs. It gives me great pleasure to thank my uncle Emmett Eiland for sharing illustrations of some of the best new rugs. The Jim Dixon Collection and the Dr. and Mrs. D. Gilbert Dumas Collections have also helped with illustrations. Dania Mallette contributed useful drawings.

I would also like to thank Indiana University, which provided me with scholarships (FLAS) to learn Georgian and Turkmen over two summers. The staff stimulated my interest in languages, settled a number of questions relating to regional fabrics, and left many lasting questions that may now be more easily answered with fieldwork.

Perhaps above all these credits I would like to thank the person who first directed me towards carpets, my father, Murray Eiland, Jr. Without his help and encouragement this project would not have been possible.

# INTRODUCTION

Most people purchase their first oriental rug before they have any notion of becoming collectors. With an acquisition destined for a particular room in the house, they may perceive that a hand-made rug will add something exotic to the décor, and after repeating the process several times they find themselves interested in a field they had never previously noticed. While still not imagining themselves as collectors, they begin to visit rug shops or to notice advertisements in magazines. Even after the third or fourth purchase they may still feel free to take rugs or leave them until a critical point is reached, and all the home's available floor space is covered. Some stop at this point and never take the step of becoming collectors. Others continue to look.

With the first purchase of a rug for the wall or perhaps a coffee table, or – and this is a serious sign – to be rolled up and stored away, the full syndrome appears. Initially these incipient collectors may take refuge in the claim that, while they may not be experts, they know what they like. But even this stance tends to waver as they begin to recognise that what seemed most appealing at first soon begins to seem mundane. An awareness dawns that some appreciate the oriental carpet as a fine art, and then an understanding emerges that, in many rug weaving parts of the world, the carpet is seen by the culture at large – not just rug dealers and those connected with the business – as the highest form of artistic expression. This revelation tends to raise the level of enthusiasm, prodding the novice collector to search for knowledge.

The quest is often not straightforward, for there are many sources of information that are far from disinterested. There are a great deal of extremely knowledgeable and honest rug dealers, but their interest usually lies in selling rather than giving information. There are also those whose enthusiasm for rugs has led to books focused on symbolism or a mystical approach to 'treasures of the East'.

Fortunately, the field is open to rational analysis, and it is possible to acquire a general orientation that can assist one in identifying rugs as to general categories and to assess a rug's qualities. It is with this goal in mind that the author has assembled the material in this book, providing a mixture of information about rugs that should give the novice a basic understanding that will help in identifying the origins of most oriental rugs.

As most collectors of oriental rugs expand their horizons to include tent and animal trappings and decorative bags made by the people who weave rugs, these items will also be discussed and illustrated. Some of these fabrics are in pile weave, while others appear in a variety of pileless weaves. Throughout this work the author will emphasise the importance of both design and the manner in which a rug is made – its structure – as they relate to identification. The territory that must be traversed extends from North Africa to the eastern-most parts of Asia, but it is a journey well worth the effort.

## The history of oriental rugs

In any field of art an understanding of the technical aspects and the evolution of designs necessarily requires that one work within a chronological framework. There are also questions as to how a given artistic medium arose and how it developed, and this often requires historical considerations.

There are several approaches one may take toward the history of the oriental carpet. Probably the most popular is that positing the carpet as a utilitarian item of household furnishing that arose on the great Eurasian steppe as a means of providing warmth, either as a floor covering or for making sleep more comfortable. It could thus be seen as a replacement for animal pelts, which were probably used by earlier hunter-gatherers. Possibly the earliest rugs would simply employ knotted pile for its use as insulation rather than as a medium for design. When this began is a matter for speculation, although it probably occurred at about the same time that mankind changed from animal hide clothing to garments fashioned from woven fabrics. It is easy to imagine a history of knotted pile going back thousands of years.

The other approach to the origin of the carpet focuses on Mesopotamia, in third-millennium-B.C. Sumer and Babylon, where records in cuneiform writing on clay tablets describe thick fabrics requiring that the surface be clipped. These were objects of trade, although the written descriptions leave some doubt as to just how they were constructed. We may derive a clue, however, from a number of clay and sculpted figurines that have survived. Many of these show people dressed in garments that appear to be covered with long loops of pile, which may be wool. One surviving figurine shows a man holding a small sheep, and his garment and the sheep's coat have the same appearance. The surviving cuneiform texts leave suggestions that at least some of the thick fabrics with a clipped surface were made for use as garments.

Assuming this is knotted pile – which is at least plausible – we could thus trace the technique back to ancient Mesopotamia. Unfortunately, no third-millennium-B.C. knotted pile fabrics either from the steppes or Mesopotamia have survived, but, by the middle of the first millennium B.C., there are finds in Central Asia that confirm the carpet's existence. A fragment from a nomadic burial mound near Bashadar in Siberia shows asymmetrical knots and is probably datable to the fifth or sixth century B.C. A complete carpet from another nearby burial mound at Pazyryk more plausibly carries a fourth century date.

The source of the Pazyryk carpet has sparked a lively debate, with some insisting that it shows Near Eastern iconography and others imagining that it was woven in Central Asia. At the very least it confirms that carpet weaving was a highly evolved art when it was woven, as the knotting is dense and the designs well executed. For nearly the next two thousand years, however, carpet remains are scarce. Fragments from the first millennium A.D. have been found in the Near East at the archaeological sites of Dura Europus in Syria and the At Tar Caves in Iraq. Coptic Egypt also produced pile carpets in a slit-loop technique. In the Takla Makan desert a number of fragments have been found, including several complete or nearly complete carpets from the third or fourth centuries A.D.

Finds are similarly sparse for the years between 500 A.D. and 1500 A.D., although in the Ala-ad-Din Mosque in Konya – central Turkey – a number of pieces have been found that are usually dated to the thirteenth century and attributed to the Seljuks. This dating is based upon the completion of the mosque in the thirteenth century and is by no means a certainty. There are also several bird or animal carpets usually associated with western Turkey that may predate 1500.

A small number of carpets from Spain may also date before 1500.

While it seems likely that more early carpets or fragments may be found, the known remains leave only a spotty record of how carpet weaving developed, and with few exceptions all this material is in public collections.

So one should understand that the carpet art, unlike some other arts, has sparse remains from which a coherent history may be constructed. The great majority of carpets in private collections are from the eighteenth or nineteenth centuries, and most oriental carpets still to be found in the world are of relatively recent make.

### Dating rugs

Unless noted in the caption, all the rugs illustrated in this book are either from the nineteenth or twentieth century, the majority dating within the mid- to late nineteenth century. This might at first seem puzzling when one considers that books on painting, sculpture, architecture, and various decorative arts, often describe items many centuries old. Although rugs have no doubt been woven for thousands of years, they are extremely perishable when compared, for example, to a bronze sculpture or a stone building. Rugs for the most part have been utilitarian, and they wear out. They are also attacked by moths, carpet beetles, mildew, and a host of other noxious elements. Consequently the survival rate has been low, and most rugs are discarded well before they are a hundred years old.

A visitor to most places selling oriental rugs today could quite conceivably find nothing made before 1900, and only specialty rug stores would have rugs dating back well into the nineteenth century. Only the most highly specialised dealers would have a stock of rugs of greater antiquity, and this could conceivably include examples made as early as the sixteenth century. Within the last several decades, only a handful of earlier pieces have been sold at auction or by the two or three international dealers who focus only upon the most ancient rugs, and these are usually fragmentary or heavily impaired in condition.

Thus a guide to collecting oriental rugs will necessarily focus on what the prospective buyer or collector is likely to find outside museums. Assuming, however, that the rugs one is likely encounter from carpet dealers and in private homes are relatively recent, there is still good reason to consider age as a pertinent factor, and it is a complex matter involving substantial controversy among carpet scholars.

There are two factors that may help. The first is the presence of an inwoven date, usually in Arabic numerals as used in the Near Eastern countries where rugs have been woven. One may find an inscription that includes a western date, such as 1895, and this involves no problem of interpretation. The rug may have been woven in some part of the Caucasus or Turkestan that had become part of the Russian Empire. The date has been based on the Christian calender and the numbers represented in western script.

More likely, however, the date will be written in Arabic script and will be based not on the birth of Christ, but on the date of Mohammad's flight from Mecca to Medina, which occurred in 622. Such a date could appear as: ١ ٣ ٧ ٩ for example, and reading this requires that we know the following equivalent numbers:

| ٠ | ١ | ٢ | ٣ | ٤ | ٥ | ٦ | ٧ | ٨ | ٩ |
|---|---|---|---|---|---|---|---|---|---|
| 0 | 1 | 2 | 3 | 4 | 5 | 6 | 7 | 8 | 9 |

The date above could thus be read as 1379, but another step must be taken to calculate the date in the western calender. Islamic dates are based upon the lunar year, which gains one year for every 33.7 solar years. Since Islamic dates start in 622, this factor must also be considered. The date can be determined as follows:

$$\frac{1379}{33.7} = 41$$

$$1379 + 622 - 41 = 1960$$

We are thus able to date the rug as relatively recent.

The other rough guideline for dating rugs is the presence of a synthetic colour, which may or may not be problematic to determine (see Chapter 2). Since we know that the first synthetic dye was made in 1853 and that it is unlikely there was significant trade with the Near East in synthetic dyestuffs before the mid-1860s, we are on safe grounds in assuming that a rug with synthetic dyes was not likely to have been woven before that time. This guideline is useful when one encounters a rug in extremely worn condition and one is tempted to assume it is many centuries old.

The degree of wear on a rug is seldom a reliable indicator of age, as – depending on the circumstances – even a well woven rug can become heavily worn in a few decades, while rugs of similar age may have been put away in a trunk and show no traces of wear after fifty years.

Aside from using inwoven dates and recognising synthetic colours, the dating of a rug requires extensive knowledge of the type and its development. The Carbon 14 method has been used to date a relatively few rugs of art historical importance, but this has serious limitations as it is reliable only for materials over two hundred and fifty to three hundred years old. If one were testing a Turkmen rug, for example, to determine whether it was a late nineteenth century rug or one woven in the middle of the eighteenth century, the result of Carbon 14 testing could not provide evidence for a reliable conclusion. A thirteenth century rug, however, could easily be distinguished from one woven in the eighteenth century.

# CHAPTER 1

# STRUCTURE AND MATERIALS

One might assume the place to start learning to identify oriental rugs would be with design, but structure – the way yarns are woven together to form a carpet – is the most reliable means, as one may find rugs with essentially identical designs from areas separated by thousands of miles. Often the most diagnostic aspects are to be found in finer points of structure, although this approach may not appeal to those with a beginner's interest in rugs. While the author urges that this chapter be read before those dealing with the various types of rugs, it may suit some readers to defer it and skip to

Chapter 3. Not everyone wishes to become a collector, and we must remind ourselves that the oriental rug can be viewed as either a work of art or simply as a piece of interior décor.

### Looms, warp, weft and knots

In order to understand how rugs are made it is necessary to consider the loom on which the process of constructing a rug begins. The simplest form, which has probably been used by nomads and villagers for thousands of years, is a basic horizontal loom in which two beams are set in parallel on the

*Figure 1. Weaver from the Shiraz area working on a horizontal loom. Almost certainly the earliest looms were of this type, as they required only two beams held firmly apart by stakes in the ground. The warp strands extended from one beam to the next, looping under the far beam before moving back toward the first beam. While weavers in urban workshops and villages now use the more complex upright loom, even today nomadic groups often use this simple horizontal structure.*

10

ground and staked so that they will remain in place as yarn is wound around first one and then the other beam (**Figure 1**). This yarn is ordinarily undyed and is called the warp. It initially lies on two levels, with some strands emerging on one side of the beams and other threads on the opposite side, leaving a gap between them. These two planes of warp are brought together as one when the first yarn to cross the warps is inserted. These crossing yarns are called wefts, and they are ordinarily begun at one end of the loom – where the weaver initially sits – and a number are passed to stabilise the fabric so that the first row of pile can be inserted. At this point we have the beginning of a fabric in that there are yarns going from one end of the loom to the other, while weft strands cross at right angles. If one were to continue weaving in this manner, the resulting piece of cloth would leave the loom with no design and be seen as a cloth of simple plain weave.

Instead, the weaver inserts segments of coloured yarn in rows across the fabric making a design in pile. These segments of pile, usually wrapped around two warps, are called knots, and there are two basic types used today. The first type is now usually called the symmetrical knot (**Figure 2**), although it is also

Figure 3. The asymmetrical knot is shown here with all warps on the same level and only one weft between the rows of knots. This does not form the kind of structure that would remain in place on its own, but the closeness of the warp strands and the other segments of pile yarn hold the knot in place.

known as the Turkish or Gördes knot, and it is used almost exclusively in Turkey, the Caucasus, among some Turkmen and Iranian tribal groups, and in the cities and towns of north-western Iran. The weaver usually has balls of yarn within reach so that knots of different colours may be tied, as the design requires, across the width of the fabric. The pile yarn is cut with a knife the weaver holds in one hand. At times a hook is used as an aide in forming the knots, which are usually tied one horizontal row at a time.

The other kind of knot is known as the asymmetrical knot, also called the Persian or Senneh knot, and this may be tied so that it may be open to the left or right (**Figure 3**). While this might seem like a small structural difference, at times it is important to note the direction of the knot to be able to distinguish one type of rug from another. This knot is used almost exclusively in China, India, and in parts of Iran – both among nomadic groups and in the cities. Most very finely woven rugs are asymmetrically knotted. As with the symmetrical knot, asymmetrical knots are usually tied around two warps, but there are types, known as jufti knots, that are tied around four warps. This is generally thought to be a labour-saving device and may be a feature used to distinguish one type of rug from another. Many rugs from the Iranian Khurasan Province and from Kashmir are jufti knotted.

Figure 2. Here the symmetrical knot is shown with two wefts (in the diagram as horizontal shoots) between the rows of knots. In this example all the warps (here appearing vertically) are on the same level, but in some rugs every other warp may be displaced away from the weaver. The trailing end of a ball of yarn is fashioned into the knot and then is cut, leaving two ends extending upward from the surface of the rug and forming the pile.

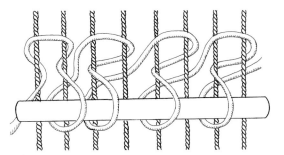

Figure 4. The pile of Tibetan rugs is not formed by tying individual knots, but involves the use of a gauge rod over which the pile is formed by drawing the yarn behind the warps and over the rod. At some point the loops over the rod are cut by pulling a knife along a groove in the gauge rod.

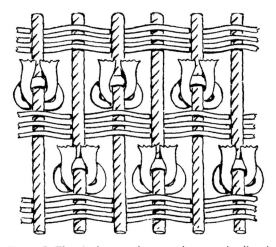

Figure 5. The single warp knot, as the name implies, is formed around a single warp and occurs in staggered rows. It is found on a few early Coptic fragments as well as on most rugs from Spain, where it is still used in a limited production of traditional-type rugs.

Tibetan rugs are made in a cut loop technique (**Figure 4**), while the classic Spanish rug was woven with staggered rows of knots tied around a single warp (**Figure 5**). Variant knots are used in parts of North Africa.

In addition to the horizontal type, there are several kinds of loom held apart by stakes driven into the ground. The most basic vertical loom is a simple frame in which the end beams are held apart by wooden side boards, and the loom is placed in an upright position so that the weavers may work seated, knotting an area in front of them rather than beneath them (**Figure 6**). The warps are placed in continuous loops around the end beams, but the weaver may work on the closest warps or may combine them to work on all the warps, the nearest and furthest, at the same time. If only the nearest warps are used, then the rug is repositioned by loosening the tension and moving the finished portion downward to expose warps not yet covered with knots. This allows the weaving of a rug nearly twice as long as the loom is high (**Figure 7**).

Another type of rug is woven on looms with roller beams above and below (**Figure 8**). In this case the completed portions of the rug are wound around the lower beam while warps may be unrolled from the upper beam. This allows rugs much longer than the loom itself to be produced.

Looms of all these types were in use centuries ago, and the only technical improvement has concerned the material from which they are made. While the looms in earlier times were all of wood, now one more frequently sees looms with metal frames and sturdier roller beam mechanisms.

Wefts, passed after each row of knots, may consist of only a single yarn (described as a shoot), between the rows of knots. Usually, however, there are at least two shoots, and use of three or more shoots between the rows of knots is not unknown. The wefts are usually passed by hand in small bundles of the material. They may be left loose or pulled tight. In the

Figure 6. Weavers working on a vertical loom in Turkmenistan. Here the weavers sit at an upright loom in which the work area where the knots are tied is shifted periodically so that the weavers will always be working directly in front of them. While looms were formerly constructed entirely of wood, modern looms are often of metal.

*Figure 7. Weavers in a Chinese rug factory in Beijing. At times many large looms are crowded into a small space, and the weavers may work in dim light. Many of the Chinese workshops are large enough to accommodate over a hundred weavers.*

*Figure 8. Kashmiri weaver working on a roller beam loom. Here a number of rugs can be woven on the loom before a new set of warps is added. This also allows rugs of virtually any length to be woven, at times even three or more times the height of the loom.*

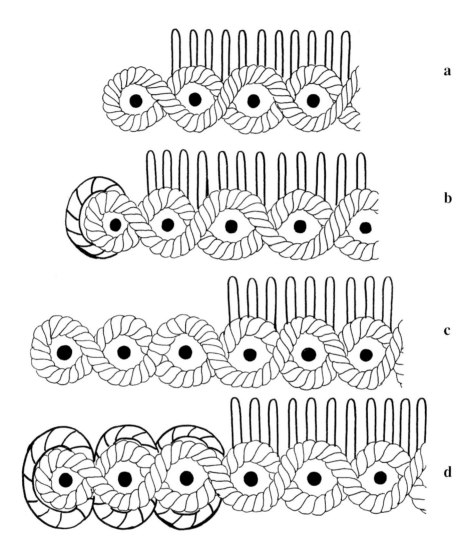

a

b

c

d

*Figure 9. The sides of a handmade rug are especially subject to wear. Figure 9a shows a simple looping of the weft around the terminal warp. This provides little protection, but an overcast of additional yarn, as in 9b, gives greater strength. Some rugs have a woven selvage in which the wefts loop in figure of eight fashion around two or more terminal warps as in 9c. This also may be reinforced with additional yarn to form a double selvage, 9d. At times the manner in which the sides are reinforced provides clues as to where the rug was woven, as the structures differ from place to place.*

latter case some distance between alternate warps is created, with the result that every other warp is slightly closer to the weaver and the alternate warp slightly further away. The two loops of the knot would then not lie exactly on the same plane, and the result would be a thicker, more inflexible fabric. Rugs in which this feature is prominent are often described as double-warped, and their relative stiffness allows them to better hold the floor without wrinkling. Most Persian city rugs are double-warped, but this feature is seldom found in Turkish or in earlier Chinese rugs.

The side finishes are usually applied while the rug is

*Figure 10. After the rug is cut from the loom, an additional clipping is done to even the pile. Here the finisher, in Amritsar, India, uses a special type of scissors specifically designed to trim the pile evenly.*

being woven on the loom, and these also may be significant in identifying where a rug was woven (**Figure 9**). At times there is a simple overcast, with the edges bound by a yarn that winds around the outer warp or group of warps. In other cases there is a selvage with yarn encircling in figure of eight fashion two or more terminal warps. This may be done by the wefts or by additional yarns, and it may be over two bundles of warps or even five or more bundles. The additional material may be the same or different from that used in the rest of the rug, and at times there are simple designs woven into it, usually in some kind of chequered pattern. There is much variation in edge finish. Baluchi rugs from eastern Iran and Afghanistan, for example, almost always show a selvage of two, three, or four cords covered with dark goat hair.

**Finishing the rug**

When the completed rug is cut from the loom, it usually requires a careful clipping to even up the pile, although the weavers will have roughly evened the pile with scissors when each row of knotting is finished. The final clipping is often done with large finishing scissors to make the pile of uniform length (**Figure 10**). The loose warp ends form the fringes at each end, or at times are woven into thick bands in order to protect the ends of the rug, which are particularly susceptible to wear. There are many local variations as to how the ends may be finished. Sometimes the warp ends are braided, while at other times one may find long bands of coloured plain weave at each end. The details of these finishes are often useful in identifying the origin of a particular rug.

## Materials

Wool is most commonly used for the pile and is also often used as a foundation material. Usually it may be identified by touch and seldom presents a diagnostic problem. When in doubt a small amount can be burned, yielding a pungent smell of burning hair. Cotton also is usually identifiable by feel and, when burnt, smells like burning paper. Silk is recognisable by touch, although one may find mercerised cotton used as a silk substitute on some modern Turkish rugs.

In the rural villages of Iran and Turkey, the weavers have often used the material they produce themselves from their flocks for both pile and foundation. Cotton often must be purchased from other areas, and this is an additional expense in a cash poor economy. City rugs are more likely to have cotton for both warp and weft, and wool for the pile is purchased from those who raise sheep in the countryside.

## Examining a rug

Throughout this book, groups of rugs will be differentiated based upon the materials used and their structure. In order to make best use of this information, it is important to be able to examine a rug to determine how it is made and what it is made of. One can begin by identifying whether the warp is wool, cotton or silk, and this can be done by examining the fringe. The material of the weft is more difficult to determine, as in an intact rug it will to some degree be buried within the body of the rug, but it can often be seen by folding the rug perpendicularly to the warps and noting the number and composition of weft strands between the rows of knots. It may be a different or the same material as the warp. Also at the ends of the rug there may be some weft strands in a pileless band between the fringe and the body of the rug. Here the material is more easily identified than when it is buried within the body of the rug.

Pile material is – not surprisingly – easier to identify, though it can vary from place to place. Some rugs use patches of cotton for the white highlights, and this is frequently encountered in several Turkish types of rug, particularly earlier rugs from the vicinity of Gördes. Other rugs have parts of the design outlined in silk, and this is particularly common on Persian Nain rugs of the last fifty years

and on certain Persian-design rugs from Kashmir. Pile wool may be soft or coarse. Imported wool used in some Pakistani rugs is often extremely soft, while much of the wool on rugs from North Africa has a particularly coarse feel.

It is worth noting the structure of the rug, particularly the knot, which often helps make an identification as to country. The number of times the weft crosses between the rows of knots may be diagnostic, and the degree to which alternate warps are depressed is also important. Recognising these features takes practice and may require the use of a magnifying glass. It usually involves bending the rug in such a way as to expose the base of the knots, although some features, such as the presence of single wefting, may easily be seen from the back of a rug.

After an careful examination of a rug, one may be able to describe it as in the following example:

*Warp*: wool, two strands.
*Weft*: wool, single strand, crosses three times between the rows of knots.
*Pile*: wool. There may be patches of silk or cotton.
*Knot*: asymmetrical, open to the right. A knot count may be given, either in knots per square inch or per square decimetre. This is obtained by multiplying the horizontal by the vertical count.
*End finish*: there are so many different types that a simple description is usually sufficient.
*Edge finish*: simple overcast or a selvage of several bundles of yarn. At times simple geometric designs are woven into the selvage. The material of the finish should also be described.

In the technical literature on oriental rugs, structural analyses are often supplied to provide the specialist with the information needed to confirm the rug's identification. In addition to the material of warp, weft, and pile, information is also often provided as to the direction in which the yarns are spun and the number of strands plied together to make up a given yarn. A yarn may thus be described as S- or Z-spun (**Figure 11**), and each strand may be plied with other strands to form a yarn. Most rug yarns are Z-spun and S-plied, although some rugs from North Africa, particularly Morocco, may have S-spun wool yarns.

## Machine-made rugs

While the author recognises that there are those who do not wish to become involved with the technical aspects of rug weaving, it may be crucial in determining the source of a rug. Also we must consider the question of distinguishing the hand-made oriental rug from the western machine-made rug in designs copied from oriental rugs. This issue often arises with those first becoming interested in rugs, and even a cursory examination of a rug can often settle the matter.

Without question there are more machine-made rugs in oriental designs sold than there are genuine hand-knotted rugs, and many department stores carry both types, often with labels and advertising that may be misleading. One should first inspect the rug to make certain that the design is also visible on the back. Some machine-made rugs show no trace of design on the underside, while there are only a few rare hand-knotted rugs that do not show the full design from the back.

A good look at the fringe will also reveal whether the threads extend from one end of the rug to the other. Often on machine-made rugs, even if the design is visible on the back, there is a strip of artificial fringe sewn on to each end.

Feeling the pile material is also important. Many inexpensive machine-made rugs have a cotton pile, which may be immediately detected by touch; the better machine-made rugs, however, may have wool pile.

There are several types of machine-made rug in which the slight ridging on the back of the rug runs across the fabric parallel with the fringe. In a genuine oriental rug the ridges will run perpendicular to the ends.

If a machine-made rug passes all these tests, then one must fold back the rug to look at the base of the pile to see whether there are traces of knots. With a little practice and reference to the previous diagrams one should be able to distinguish between the genuine oriental rug and the machine-made copy.

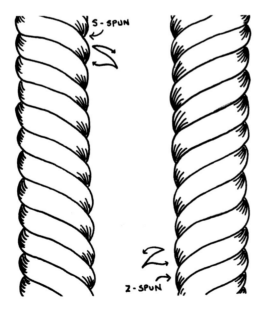

*Figure 11. Comparison diagrams of two yarns shows the different appearances given by Z- and S-spun yarns. After spinning, the strands are then twisted together to form a yarn. If the fibres are Z-spun, the yarn will be S-plied.*

# CHAPTER 2

# DESIGNS AND DYES

The designs of specific rug weaving areas will be covered in subsequent chapters, but it is useful to divide designs into broad types so that descriptions of various rugs are more easily understood. Perhaps the most important distinction is that between floral rugs with flowing lines described as curvilinear (**Figure 12**) and those with angular designs described as geometric (**Figure 13**). Curvilinear rugs are usually more finely

woven than those with geometric designs, meaning that there are more knots per given unit of measurement.

In addition to a general description of the design, one can also describe a rug in terms of the manner in which the design is organised. For example, there are rugs with a single large figure, usually symmetrical, in the centre, and these are described as medallion rugs (**Figure 14**). Other rugs show the same design motifs

*Figure 12. In this Ferahan Sarouk adaptation of a seventeenth century Persian rug, every aspect of the design is curvilinear except the lines delineating the borders. Curved lines usually require that the knotting is fine, and the effect is produced here by the fact that there are about 200 knots per square inch.*

*Figure 13. Although the design elements in this Afshar rug were probably inspired by floral or animal forms, they have here become entirely geometric. This is a result of the low knot count, with slightly over 40 knots per square inch. These figures could not have been given graceful, curved lines with such coarse knotting.*

*Figure 14. Persian Serapi rug with a medallion and pendants. The medallion has long been used in Islamic art, and it appears early in the art of the book, when medallion designs were used as frontispieces. At times the medallion was used as part of an infinite repeat, with the borders of the carpet functioning as a window allowing only a central medallion and secondary medallions at each corner to be seen.*

*Figure 15 (opposite). Afshar tribal rug with twelve elaborate boteh figures on an ivory field. The boteh may be either curvilinear or geometric and appears in a wide range of sizes. It appears on city rugs and village rugs and probably entered the Persian design lexicon via the Kashmir shawl, which may show a myriad of botehs in different shapes and sizes.*

*Figure 16 (above). Herati pattern on a Bijar rug. The herati pattern probably does not predate the eighteenth century and appears to have developed from a group of earlier red field rugs woven in India. In Persia it was popular by the early nineteenth century and appears in the finest Sennehs and some of the crudest village rugs.*

repeating over and over across the field without any kind of central organisation. The boteh, a pear-shaped motif, is common on Iranian rugs and is drawn in both curvilinear and rectilinear forms **(Figure 15)**. There may be rugs with multiple medallions and repeating designs of substantial complexity. A common repeating design is the herati **(Figure 16)**, which occurs on many nineteenth century Persian rugs and

*Figure 17 (opposite). Tekke Turkmen rug with repeating geometric figures usually called guls. Note the flatwoven bands at each end. While essentially this same design was used for at least two hundred years, and perhaps more, there are subtle differences in design details and colour that allow them to be assigned an approximate date. The earliest rugs are more likely to have four vertical rows of guls, while later rugs may have six or seven rows. Approx. 64 x 47½ins. (163 x 121cm).*

*Figure 18. This rug from the Sultanabad region shows the Persian repeating design referred to as the mustaphi, which does not seem to predate the nineteenth century. It was used mostly on rugs intended for export.*

on examples from other areas that have adopted Persian designs. Many Turkmen rugs show a repeating design made up of geometric figures **(Figure 17)**, while finely woven Persian rugs may show elaborate repeating designs with spiral vinework and realistic floral forms **(Figure 18)**.

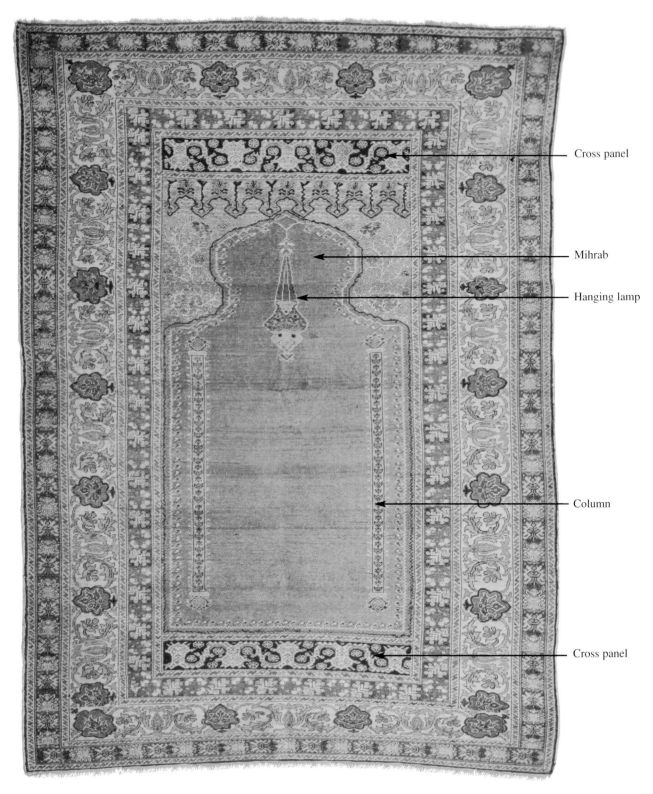

Cross panel

Mihrab

Hanging lamp

Column

Cross panel

*Figure 19 (opposite). Turkish prayer rug showing traditional mihrab, hanging lamp, and columns, with cross panels at both ends of the field. Only the mihrab is essential, as the field below the mihrab may be empty, and both the columns and cross panels may be missing. Prayer rugs woven in Persian cities are likely to be entirely floral, and it would be unusual to find animal figures on a prayer rug or any rug intended for use within a mosque.*

*Figure 20 (above). Portion of a large Ersari saff with multiple niches. These are usually found in mosques and may have more than one row of niches. Although saffs are not common, they are found in small numbers from Turkey eastward to Eastern Turkestan.*

Some rugs are pictorial, while others show a design with a niche at one end that gives it an asymmetry **(Figure 19)**. These rugs are described as prayer rugs, with an arch called a mihrab that is pointed toward Mecca during the Moslem's five-times-per-day prayers. Prayer rug designs may be either geometric or curvilinear, depending on where they are woven. A large prayer rug with multiple niches is often woven for mosques and is called a saff **(Figure 20)**.

One important design convention of the oriental rug is the division between the border and the inner portion; this is described as the field. There is usually one border, called the main border, that is wider than the others, and this is bounded by narrower minor borders or guard stripes, as they are often called. Occasionally one encounters broken borders, in which the lines are interrupted to allow the field design to encroach into the border area. One seldom finds pile rugs without borders, although many pileless fabrics or kilims (see Chapter 10) have no borders **(Figure 21)**.

### Symbolism in design

The concept that the designs of oriental rugs carry with them deeply symbolic meanings is probably less current today than it was half a century ago, but one still encounters those who insist that somehow the wisdom of the mysterious East lurks within the scrolling vines and crudely drawn animal figures of many rugs. Certainly some rugs have been woven for special purposes that communicate a meaning beneath their surface décor, and there are, of course, pictorial rugs and those with explicit inscriptions that leave the viewer with no doubt as to the designer's intent. Many times, however, a translation of the inscription is not particularly informative. It should surprise no one that some prayer rugs will occasionally be found inscribed with a verse from the Koran.

It is also clear that some of the inscriptions are little more than advertisements for their makers. Some inscriptions give the name of the merchant commissioning the rug, along with a date. At times rugs are identified as commemorating an event, such as a wedding or the birth of a son. The signature of a master weaver is also common.

More obscure are the small figures often found on rugs that some collectors describe as symbolising various animals. When one hears that a certain motif in the border of a Persian rug symbolises, or depicts in schematic form, a turtle, this does not really tell the viewer much about what that means. There are devices in many village rugs described as spiders, scorpions, and running dogs. There are even clear drawings of birds, horses and lions. Are these to be seen as decorative motifs or as deeply symbolic messages?

This author is sceptical of this approach to rug design. One can travel from village to village asking the weavers what various of the motifs in their rugs mean, and at times the simplest devices get fanciful but inconsistent labels. What is labelled as a scorpion in one village may be a device to ward off the evil eye to the next group of weavers.

### The appeal of older rugs

To the novice collector the search for rugs of progressively older age often seems peculiar, particularly as older rugs are more likely to be heavily worn. And do the differences in design, when they exist, mean that the older rug is necessarily better?

There are reasons to question the concept that old is good and new is bad, but there is often some truth behind the concept. In taking a historical view, one can recognise that the sixteenth and seventeenth centuries in many respects represent the artistic highpoint of the Islamic world in the Middle East and on the Indian subcontinent. At that time the Ottoman Empire reached its zenith and extended across North Africa and so far into south-eastern Europe that Vienna was besieged twice by Turkish armies. Great mosques and palaces were built in Istanbul and elsewhere in the empire, and artisans were supported by the enormous wealth of the imperial court.

At the same time Persia saw the artistic flowering of the Safavids, with the construction of the great mosques and palaces of Isfahan, and the appearance of lavish workshops for luxury goods working directly for the Shah. Persian art reached its high point of achievement, building upon centuries of craftsmanship and creativity. Partially borrowing from the Safavid achievement, the Moghul dynasty, in what is now India and Pakistan, amassed enormous wealth and similarly endowed a lavish building programme, including the Taj Mahal, and imported artists and craftsmen from as far away as Europe.

These centuries set the standard for their respective cultures, but as the dynasties declined in world importance, the artistic flowering of these

---

*Figure 21. Many flatwoven rugs, like this example from the Fethiye region of Turkey, have designs with no borders. An arrangement like this is rare on a pile rug. The colours are typical of western Anatolia. Approx. 121 x 58ins. (308 x 147cm).*

27

extravagant times seems also to have declined. A lavish prayer rug for the Ottoman court of the sixteenth century, for example, would be copied in the next century even in the provinces, although it would not be so finely woven, and elements of the design would be simplified. By the eighteenth century the basic design format would appear even in village rugs, but now there would be a greater simplification, and perhaps some aspects of the design would be grossly misunderstood by the weaver. By the nineteenth century a design that began with a graceful arch and columns, with a hanging lamp in the arch, would have become so simplified that the hanging lamp might have disappeared entirely, and the floral forms reduced to geometric abstractions.

The point I am trying to make is that, from the perspective of the collector seeking the purest expression of a particular artistic style, the later rugs may seem crude and degenerate in design. From this perspective older is better, and the more recent prayer rugs based on Ottoman court models may seem crude and graceless.

At the same time, other collectors may find the later village version of an Ottoman design more vigorous and possessing a certain life that the court rug lacks. In this case the more the design has evolved away from its court origin, the more it is appreciated. On one point both types of collectors would agree, however. Both would see the most recent rugs, particularly from the twentieth century, as lacking a spirit either of the court or of an intact rural culture. The recent rugs would more likely have lost any spark of creativity and simply represent the emotionless output of standardised designs for the market. Many recent rugs appear to have been woven by weavers who had no particular pride of accomplishment or sense that a rug represented anything of themselves.

So there are many different opinions on the designs of rugs, with some collectors preferring court-derived designs and others more enthusiastic about village or nomadic rugs. Currently the pendulum has swung in the direction of rugs with a rural derivation, although the Iranians who collect rugs often prefer the court-inspired city rugs.

## Dyes

Two major categories of dye are used in the materials found in oriental rugs, traditional and synthetic.

Traditional dyes all derive from naturally occurring substances.

In the Near East indigo, from a plant growing wild in some areas but usually as a cultivated crop in others, is the main source of all shades of blue, and it has been found on the earliest surviving textiles from several millennia ago. Its application is a complicated process, but the colour is fast to water and fades little. On some early Chinese rugs one may find as many as four different shades of indigo blue. In areas where it is not grown, it is obtained through trade.

There are two basic sources of red. The root of the madder plant, which also grows wild but is mainly cultivated, and dyes made from the powdered bodies of dried scale insects. Madder is most common and provides a variable red that often appears as a deep brick red or a rust colour. It may be intense, but is seldom bright, and it blends well with indigo. Among the insect dyes, lac from India and cochineal, originally from Mexico but now grown in the Canary Islands and North Africa, are most common. They are related and give similar shades of red that range from a cooler shade with a blue component to a bright scarlet. Part of the variation comes from the mordant, a substance that helps bind the dye to the yarn. Alum is the most common mordant where rugs are woven, and variations in its mineral content give madder red some regional variations.

Yellows are usually obtained from a variety of locally grown plants. *Delphinium semibarbatum*, called by various names in the Near East, gives a strong yellow, as does the vine weld, but there are numerous others. A yellow dyebath after wool has been dyed with indigo yields a good green, usually with a little mottling so that one can see traces of both components. Yellow with madder or an insect dye can give various shades of orange.

Purple, which is relatively rare on naturally dyed rugs, usually involves using an indigo and a red dye.

The brown or brown-black in oriental rugs has often proved problematic. It is probably most satisfactory when naturally dark wool is used, but there are times when brown/black is dyed with gall

*Figure 22. Persian Malayer rug showing prominent abrash in the field. While this feature is usually attributable to the use of small dye lots, it often makes the design more interesting. Modern rugs, particularly those dyed exclusively with synthetic dyes, seldom show significant abrash, but the feature has become prominent again among the new generation of naturally-dyed rugs.*

nuts, walnut husks, or other vegetal sources in which iron is a substantial component. Often yarns with these dyes wear more rapidly than other yarns, leaving the black – which is usually employed for outlining – somewhat lower than the other colours.

Many older rugs show a feature described as abrash. This refers to the variation in a single colour over the entirety of the rug (**Figure 22**). A blue field colour, for example, could be quite different at one end of the field than the other, and often it could be seen to vary substantially in horizontal bands throughout the rug. The most likely explanation for this is the use of small dye lots, which even with the same dye would give slightly different results from one batch to the next. It is likely that the differences have often become more pronounced as the colours aged. Most collectors see this as a positive rather than negative feature, as it often provides an added dimension to the design. Abrash is more common on village and nomadic rugs than on city rugs, in which the colours were often dyed by professional dyers in larger lots and consequently show less variation.

Ordinarily the back of an older rug shows brighter colours than the front, as light causes some fading of even the best natural dyes. Occasionally one finds the opposite effect, with a more intensely coloured surface. Some of these rugs have had one or more colours painted on to the surface in order to have their overall effect changed to better meet market demands **(Figure 23)**.

Starting in the 1850s the laboratories of Europe began to synthesize artificial dyes. Natural substances were relatively expensive and often difficult to apply. As a result synthetics rapidly spread into most parts of the world, at times into areas that at first glance would appear to be beyond the easy reach of western trade. From an artificial magenta first discovered in 1853, a series of colours were synthesized, and these quickly spread to the textile industry. Other colours followed in quick succession, but the problem was that a number of them proved unstable in water and caused colour-run in a wet fabric. Others faded rapidly, and some faded into tones that were quite different from the original colour.

Initially these dyes spread rapidly before their defects were fully recognised, and by the time there was a strong reaction against them they had established a firm foothold. By 1900 most rugs exported from the Near East were at least partially synthetically dyed, and by the end of the Second World War there was little natural dyeing. In many places the art had died out, and rugs coming to the West had a different look to them than those of fifty years before.

Over time synthetic dyes improved to the point where many were stable in water, and the quality of the colours improved. By the 1960s, when the oriental rug began to rapidly increase in popularity, the new rugs generally available were those using synthetic dyes, which prompted many to pay particularly large sums for older rugs with natural dyes. At that time a small movement advocating the return to natural dyeing began (see pp.178–180).

Those buying a rug who want to make certain that the example they are interested in is naturally dyed can never be certain by a visual inspection alone, although there are clues that can suggest certain dyes are synthetic. The ultra-bright pink and orange colours on some recent rugs are unlikely to be products of natural dyes, and excessive fading of any particular colour suggests that it was not produced with a natural dye.

Blue is the least likely colour to provide information about the dye used, as it usually comes either from natural or synthetic indigo, which are chemically the same and thus cannot be distinguished. There are some other synthetic blues, including one that leaves a bright blue on the back of the rug but fades to a greyish colour on the front.

Reds are most problematic, as faulty red synthetic dyes are among those most likely to run when the rug is wet. The quality of the weave is no guarantee that the red will be fast to water, and this author has seen even well-woven Isfahan rugs of the 1960s in which the reds have run and given all the white areas of the rug a pinkish cast. One should check closely for colour run and compare the back and front of the rug to see whether the front shows excessive fading from light.

*Figure 23. Sarouk rug with detached floral sprays. The field has been painted to change the shade of red, and the rug would appear lighter on the back. Such designs are directed toward the American market and have little to do with Persian art.*

**24**

*Figures 24, 25, and 26. Three pairs of rug details similar in either design or point of origin. The pieces on the left have natural colours, and their counterparts on the right show synthetic colours.*

*Figure 24 shows two Turkish yastiks, with the rug on the right showing synthetic colours often found in the 1960s, while that on the left shows a range of natural colours typical of the Konya region during the nineteenth century.*

*Figure 25 shows two examples of weaving from the Shiraz area, with a nineteenth century Khamseh carpet on the left contrasted with a 1970s Qashqa'i sampler on the right.*

*Figure 26 shows similar portions of two Chinese rugs, left a mid-nineteenth century chair cover, and right a 1970s silk rug.*

*The intent here is to show that with natural dyes there are often substantial differences that give the rug a more harmonious tonality.*

**Figures 24, 25 and 26** illustrate three pairs of rug details that are similar in design or point of origin. The examples on the left have natural colours, and those on the right show synthetic colours.

The intent here is not to imply that telling the difference between natural and synthetic colours is a simple, obvious matter, but that there are often substantial differences that give the rug a more harmonious tonality with natural dyes. No doubt the colours in all the naturally-dyed examples were originally more intense, but they have mellowed into an appealing harmony. In each of these pairs the synthetic colours are unlikely ever to look more appealing than they do at present.

25

26

# CHAPTER 3

# PERSIAN RUGS

There is some confusion over the word Persian as it refers to oriental rugs. The country known as Persia changed its name to Iran in the 1920s, but by that time the term 'Persian rug' had become something of a generic name for any hand-made pile rug from the Near East. Rugs from Iran are still often referred to as Persian, and in this book both terms will be used.

Iran serves as a good example of the differences between city rugs and those made by villagers and nomads. While rugs were woven there for at least several millennia, apparently only fragments dating before 1500 survive, although this is a matter of controversy. Rugs are often extremely difficult to date, although three dated carpets from the Safavid dynasty (1500–1721) bear woven inscribed dates, including the pair of carpets found at the Shrine of Ardabil with a date of 1539/40. The most complete of these carpets is currently in the Victoria and Albert Museum in London, while another early Persian carpet, inscribed with the date most plausibly read as 1522/23 is in the Poldi Pezzoli Museum in Milan. Other carpets surviving from the early Safavid period include three large silk carpets of an extremely fine weave, with two of them ranging around 700 asymmetrical knots per square inch. These carpets, which include large examples in Vienna and Boston, are plausibly dated stylistically to the early sixteenth century and associated with the Safavid court of Shah Ismail or Shah Tahmasp.

While hundreds of carpets survive from the Safavid era, there is still controversy as to where many of them were made. Tabriz, the first Safavid capital, was almost certainly a source, while the subsequent capital in Isfahan is known to be a source. European travellers of the seventeenth century describe the exact location of the carpet workshops, and there is documentation of carpet weaving in Kashan at about the same time. Kerman was also a major source of carpets in a wide variety of designs, including a type characterised by realistically drawn blossoms in a lattice framework in which vases may be found. There is also good reason to believe that carpets were woven in Herat, which was part of the Persian Empire during Safavid times.

After the Safavid collapse, there seems to have been a decline in rug production, although it certainly continued for local use. Safavid designs had became part of an enduring design lexicon that has lasted up to the present, with elaborate, stylised palmettes, scrolling vinework, complex medallions, and multiple lattice systems. Many of these same motifs resurfaced in the nineteenth century when the country began again to produce rugs in quantity to meet international demand.

## PERSIAN CITY RUGS

Persian city rugs have a number of features in common, including use of the asymmetrical knot on a cotton foundation in which the wefts usually cross twice between the rows of knots. They are finely woven, ranging from about 110 to over 600 knots per square inch, and their designs are ordinarily curvilinear and floral, with motifs adapted from rugs of the Safavid period. They are typically designed by specialists, with wool processed by professional dyers. Weaving today is carried out by young women and children, though in the Safavid period men were also employed. Most city rugs are double-warped which makes them rather inflexible (**Figure 27**). Basic designs of the Persian city rug are widely copied from China to the Balkans, India and Pakistan in particular have been borrowers of Persian designs.

---

*Figure 27. This late nineteenth century Tabriz rug with a typical medallion design, is characteristic of most Persian city rugs in being double-warped and consequently rather inflexible. While it resembles other Persian city rugs, it can be distinguished by its symmetrical knotting, which varies greatly in density from the coarsest to the finest rugs. The wool usually has a harsher feel than rugs of Mashhad, Kerman, or Kashan.*

*Tabriz*

Merchants from Tabriz took the lead in organising the rug industry in Iran when it revived in the last half of the nineteenth century, for Tabriz lies relatively close to Istanbul, the major shipping point to Europe. As demand from the West grew, these dealers first organised a system by which old rugs from the bazaars were channelled to Tabriz for subsequent shipment abroad. When the supplies of old rugs proved insufficient for the demand, these same merchants were instrumental in other parts of Persia in encouraging the expansion of local rug industries.

While there had been a low level of rug production in the Tabriz area, possibly extending centuries into the past, the new demand also brought about an expansion of the local industry which began to produce a type of rug that became recognisable throughout the western world. The Tabriz carpet followed the tradition of using cotton for the warp and weft, while the pile wool has a rather harsh feel. The designs most frequently included medallions and often showed adaptations of Safavid motifs **(Figure 28)**. These carpets differ from other Persian city carpets in being woven with the symmetrical knot.

*Figure 28 (opposite). Tabriz rugs occur in a wide variety of designs and may have either silk or wool pile. This is probably a late nineteenth century piece with a design that could well have come from another Persian city.*

*Figure 29 . Late nineteenth century Kashan in a medallion design. The medallion of Kashan rugs is often smaller than that found on Tabriz or Kerman rugs, and the drawing is somewhat stiffer than that of the Tabriz medallion rug in Figure 28.*

From the first decades of the revival, the workshops in Tabriz have been adept at modelling their carpets to meet western demands, changing the colour schemes and designs as needed to gain market advantage. There are many grades of Tabriz carpet including some of the finest and some of the coarsest city types.

A group of silk rugs from the late nineteenth and early twentieth centuries was woven in Tabriz, and one occasionally sees examples at auction going for steep prices. The designs were often borrowed, at times from early Turkish prayer rugs.

## Kashan and Qum

The cities of Kashan and Qum are often discussed together, as their rugs share the typical structure of the Persian city rug, and their designs are similar. While weaving in Kashan is documented during Safavid times, it is unclear whether there has been an unbroken tradition. Kashan rugs from the last half of the nineteenth century are known, usually in medallion designs (**Figure 29**). By the end of the nineteenth century Kashan rugs were among the most consistently finely knotted of all Persian rugs, and it was only half a century later that the rugs of Isfahan

*Figure 30. This finely woven prayer rug shows the elaborate design and complex major border typical of early twentieth century Kashan. Such rugs are increasingly sought by collectors of city rugs. Approx. 82 x 51½ins. (208 x 131cm).*

and Nain came to exceed them in the number of knots per square inch.

Silk has long been produced in the Kashan area, and a number of early Kashans were all silk. A late nineteenth/early twentieth century type of Kashan was made with merino wool from Australia or New Zealand, spun in England, and these rugs are described as having 'Manchester wool' **(Figure 30)**. Later Kashans have a wool indistinguishable from that of other Persian city rugs.

Medallion designs have remained common on Kashan rugs, often on a red field with relatively small lozenge-shaped medallions. Prayer rug designs are also encountered, and occasionally one encounters a pictorial Kashan. Kashans of the last several decades often show a colour scheme based around ivory, blue, and beige.

The industry in Qum has mirrored that of nearby Kashan, although modern production appears to have begun several decades later, and there was no tradition of rug weaving there during Safavid times. Many of the smaller pieces are in prayer rug designs, while a number of Qum silks appear in a so-called garden design in which the field is divided into squarish compartments, each with a variety of floral figures.

Both Kashan and Qum rugs range from about 140 to over 300 knots per square inch, with the silk pieces often being finer. Both types enjoy high status in local and western markets.

There are several towns near Kashan, most prominently Aroon, that weave Kashan designs in a slightly lower grade.

*Isfahan and Nain*
While Isfahan was a producer of rugs for the Safavid court in the seventeenth century, the art seems to have died out there until it was revived in the first quarter of the twentieth century. The Isfahan is among the finer Persian city rugs, ranging between about 250 to above 600 asymmetrical knots per square inch. Finely woven rugs may have a silk foundation, and a number of them have an inwoven signature of the master weaver, often in a small patch of pile weave at one end. Silk Isfahans also often show hunting scenes. Medallions are common, often on a red field, although there are also intricate repeating designs **(Figure 31)**.

*Figure 31. Finely woven rug from Isfahan in an unusual directional medallion design. Medallion designs are much the most common from Isfahan, but there are also a small number of repeating and pictorial designs.*

In many respects Isfahan represents the centre of Safavid art, with many surviving mosques and several palaces associated with the lavish imperial court of the seventeenth century. With such inspiration locally

*Figure 32. Mid-twentieth century rug from Nain, with the design elements outlined in ivory silk and unusually fine asymmetrical knotting. Although Nain designs are based around Safavid motifs, the history of carpet weaving in this city extends back little more than half a century.*

1940s. Nains average an even higher knot count than Isfahans, and they frequently have the outlines of floral figures woven in ivory silk, giving additional highlights to the rug. Later Nains often have a colour scheme based around ivory, blue, and beige, with less red than the typical Isfahan (**Figure 32**).

*Kerman*

The Kerman rug has an unusual structure. There are three wefts between the rows of knots, with two of them pulled tightly to place the warps on two levels. Most rugs of the Safavid period from various parts of the country were woven in this manner, but, interestingly, the feature survives among asymmetrically knotted rugs only in Kerman.

The rugs of Kerman are noted for excellent wool, which makes for a bright white rather than the usual darker ivory. Red colours were long based on insect dyes, a characteristic shared only with the rugs of Mashhad and other cities of Khurasan. Kermans show an enormous variability in design, as designers are artisans of substantial status there. Foreign firms gained control of many Kerman looms late in the nineteenth century, and most of the rugs were consequently directed toward western markets, particularly American. These included a number of rugs of unusual size, and when one finds an early twentieth century rug over 18 feet (5.5 metres) long it is likely to be a Kerman. Medallion designs have been most common, with elaborate floral motifs covering the field (**Figure 33**).

The standard Kerman weave remained in the vicinity of about 140 knots per square inch for decades, although there have always been finer pieces ranging to over 300 knots per inch.

By the second quarter of the twentieth century these rugs seemed to lose something of their Persian character, as the pile was made longer and the designs simpler. As the mid-twentieth century approached, open fields with attenuated pastel colours and French style broken borders became increasingly common. During the last several decades the Kerman rug has reverted to

accessible, it is not surprising that these early designs have been particularly prominent on Isfahan rugs.

A lower grade rug, resembling the Isfahan and also usually in medallion designs, is made in the town of Najafabad.

The rugs of Nain resemble those of Isfahan, although weaving may not have begun there until the

*Figure 33. Multiple medallion Kerman rug, possibly as early as the mid-nineteenth century. Occasionally one finds a rug of this type exceeding 30 feet (9 metres) in length.*

42

*Figure 34 (opposite). Kerman prayer rug with animal figures in addition to the vase and flowers. This example shows the colour scheme typical of Kerman, with cochineal reds rather than the brick-red colours obtained with madder. Since most Kermans of the last several decades were destined for the American market, they also showed a slightly different approach to design. Approx. 84 x 49ins. (213 x 125cm).*

*Figure 35 (above). Kerman pictorial rug in an unusual round format. Weaving a round rug imposes no particular technical problem for the weaver. The first row of knots would be short, and the longest rows would occur at the middle. Approx. 35ins. (89cm) diameter.*

earlier traditions to appeal to the local Iranian market. The colours are brighter, and the designs follow those of earlier rugs **(Figures 34 and 35)**.

A number of pictorial Kermans are known, along with pieces in prayer rug designs, usually with a central tree and at times with animal and bird figures. All sizes are woven from small mats to giant rugs.

Several other cities in the vicinity of Kerman have long produced a similar type of rug that is usually sold in the West under the Kerman label. The ancient city of Yazd, on the edge of the Great Desert, has a long tradition of rug weaving. Its products resemble the Kerman, although regional output has not been so consistently directed toward western markets. Mahan and Ravar also have produced Kerman-type rugs, and at times the most finely woven Kermans are given a Ravar label.

*Mashhad, Birjand and Qain*

Like the Kerman, which they often outwardly resemble, these types have cooler reds from insect dyes, although they have a structural peculiarity that sets them apart. Here the jufti asymmetrical knot is endemic, and the rugs, which are woven with a particularly soft wool from the area, are less durable than most other Persian city rugs. As the jufti involves tying the asymmetrical knot over four warps rather than two, the resulting fabric is less resistant to wear. Medallion designs are particularly common, although many nineteenth century examples show repeating designs.

Rugs from Mashhad are also unusual in that the region produces rugs with asymmetrical jufti knots along with symmetrically knotted types. The latter tradition probably began with Tabrizi merchants in the late nineteenth century, when they established a weaving industry in Mashhad modelled on that of Tabriz. Rugs of both types may show the same designs, including many prayer rugs and pictorial carpets **(Figure 36)**. Several workshops in Mashhad became particularly well known during the first quarter of the twentieth century, and – although their output was limited – some of their rugs were extremely finely woven with complex floral designs.

Rugs from the Birjand and Qain areas are consistently asymmetrically jufti knotted, traditionally using red shades based around lac or cochineal, and it is often difficult to tell recent examples apart **(Figure 37)**. During the late nineteenth century, however, each of these areas, as well as the town of Doruksh, produced a distinct type of rug. Floral repeating designs were popular, but medallion designs are now most common, often in standard room sizes. Quality is variable from relatively coarse to extremely

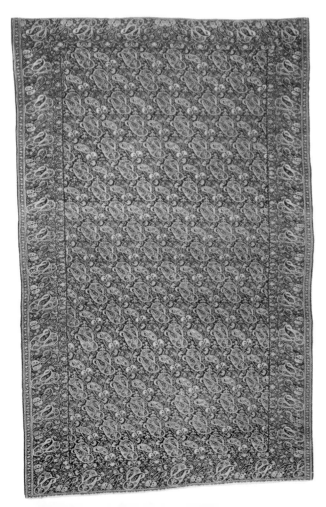

*Figure 36 (opposite). Unusual Mashhad pictorial rug with a horse and rider and tree. The design here is based upon many found on Persian miniature paintings of previous centuries. Like the rugs of Kerman, Mashhad rugs of the last several decades also showed a cochineal red. Approx. 91½ x 62½ins. (232 x 159cm).*

*Figure 37. Rug with repeating boteh figures from the vicinity of Qain in Khurasan. The reds in this type of rug are dyed with cochineal. The jufti knot is standard. While the type was popular during the late nineteenth century, they were made with soft wool that did not wear well. Consequently few of them have survived, and their designs are not now so stylish as they once were.*

fine. Nowhere is this better exemplified than in the town of Mud, near Birjand. Here a medium grade medallion rug has been produced in great numbers, and these often appear in the West. Much less common is a small group of extremely fine, well-designed Mud rugs.

## Arak

The area around Arak (formerly Sultanabad) has woven something of a hybrid between the Persian city rug and village rugs. Most of the production is from surrounding towns and villages, and the rugs range from fine to medium density, with the asymmetrical knot on cotton foundations. They may show elaborate curvilinear designs, although not usually involving Safavid motifs.

Many rugs from the last half of the nineteenth century have survived, and many of these pieces from the Arak area show designs with rather stiff medallions. These were usually labelled as Sarouks, although such pieces were woven in many places other than the town of that name (**Figure 38**). Another

*Figure 38 (opposite left). Late nineteenth century Sarouk medallion rug with an ivory field and gracefully drawn botehs in the corners. These rugs were well dyed and well woven, and they covered a wide range of sizes up to examples exceeding 20 feet (6 metres) in length.*

*Figure 39 (opposite right). Late nineteenth century Sarouk medallion rug with an ivory field and elaborate pendants. Comparison with the example in Figure 38 reveals the enormous variety available within the format of the medallion rug.*

*Figure 40. Late nineteenth century Sarouk rug, also showing the variability of the simple medallion format.*

type of rug from the district was sold in the West under the Ferahan label, and these typically had repeating designs, often the herati. Most had a blue ground colour and an appealing light green colour in the border.

Early in the twentieth century, many rugs from this area were made under the direction of foreign firms, and the output was directed towards the West. These pieces were carefully designed from traditional Persian motifs, using colours suited to western tastes, and avoiding the bright reds favoured in Iran. The rugs were usually marketed under names reflecting their grade rather than a specific town or village of origin.

Sarouk was the name given to the highest grade, whether the particular carpet was woven in the town of that name or a number of other places that produced the same kind of carpet. Unlike the turn-of-the century Sarouk, with its rather stiff medallion design of a type probably adapted from early Tabriz carpets, the field was usually covered with detached floral sprays, usually on a red ground. It was tightly woven and ranged from about 100 to 200 knots per square inch (**Figures 39 and 40**). The Sarouk was popular in the United States during the 1920s and 1930s. Before they were sold, these rugs were often bleached and the reds repainted with a maroon dye, giving them a darker appearance. They are thus

*Figure 41. Large rug from the Arak region. The design is made up of a combination of classic Persian motifs. Clearly it is a commercial rug, probably made for a European or American firm, but the colours are harmonious, and the design is consistent with a Persian origin. Approx. 132 x 111ins. (336 x 282cm).*

unusual in showing a darker red colour on the front than on the back. One would expect the exact opposite, as it is usually the front surface of the rug that fades, but in these cases, the colour painted on to the surface was usually darker than the original red.

Mahal is usually used as a label for lower grades from the Arak district. Most were woven under controlled conditions and are of good quality, although they are not finely knotted. Colours are usually excellent, with little abrash. They are based around classic Persian patterns with elements created specifically for western markets **(Figure 41)**. At times these rugs are sold under the Ziegler label, from a major foreign-owned firm in Arak that controlled many looms and was a major exporter to Europe.

## IRANIAN TOWN AND VILLAGE RUGS

There is a group of rugs made in the countryside in Iran by villagers who either raise sheep or purchase their

*Figure 42. Very fine Senneh with the typical narrow borders and fine design of small repeated figures. The feel of the Senneh is unusual in that it has some depression of alternate warps and only one weft between the rows of knots. That means that one lateral half of every symmetrical knot is depressed, but the knots on surrounding rows are depressed the in opposite way. This gives the rug a rough feel on the back. Approx. 73½ x 47½ins. (187 x 121cm).*

wool from neighbouring nomadic groups. Their rugs resemble neither the city rugs nor are they like the rugs woven by nomads. Examples from the nineteenth century are usually woven on an all-wool foundation, as this was available from local production. Cotton has come into wider use in the last century, and the knotting may be either symmetrical or asymmetrical, most often the former, and the rugs are woven in a variety of shapes and sizes. For the most part, however, the largest room-sized rugs are woven in Iranian cities.

The Kurds in particular have produced a wide range of village rugs, although the finest Kurdish rugs, from the city of Senneh (now called Sanandaj) are something of a hybrid between city and village **(Figure 42)**. They may have extremely short pile, fine weave, and cotton foundation with only one weft shoot between the rows of knots. Although some of the older rug books describe the asymmetrical knot as a Senneh knot, the rugs from this city are symmetrically knotted. Designs of the Senneh include

*Figure 43. This small Bijar rug is shaped to cover a saddle, and like other Kurdish rugs from this area is particularly thick. While the Senneh is, for the most part woven within the city, the Bijar is woven in several dozen nearby villages and in the city of Bijar. Consequently there is much more variation in the designs and textures of the rugs.*

fine renditions of the herati and repeating boteh figures. There are some medallion designs, which are far less curvilinear than the standard Persian city rug. The finest Sennehs may have silk warps, at times in bands of different colours. It is likely that rugs were woven in Senneh well before the late nineteenth century expansion of rug weaving, as some examples with early inscribed dates are known.

A group of villages around the Kurdish town of Bijar weave an entirely different type of rug known for its rigidity. These rugs often – but not always – have three thick wefts between the rows of knots, with alternate warps pushed into different levels making them double-warped. The range of designs includes the classic Persian herati, but there are also many medallion rugs, some with bold arabesque leaf designs

(**Figures 43 and 44**). These rugs are extremely durable and some are very large. A number of 'sampler' rugs are known from Bijar, where they were apparently used as something analogous to pattern books. In a small rug the entire design lexicon of a larger rug could be represented, although these pieces often lacked design symmetry.

Hundreds of other Kurdish villages in western Iran also produce rugs of a more generic type, usually with wool foundations with a rather loose weave. The designs include those used by Senneh and Bijar, but the variation is somewhat greater. Many rugs show a repeat of simple geometric figures. A number of long narrow rugs, called runners in the West, are made in Kurdish villages. The wool of these rugs is ordinarily of an excellent quality (**Figure 45**).

*Figure 44. Bijar medallion rug with an unusually narrow border. The prominent use of yellow is, for some reason, common on many late nineteenth century Bijars.*

*Figure 45. Kurdish village rug from western Iran. These pieces are all wool and appear in a variety of sizes with traditional Persian designs. Often they cannot be specifically localised, but they are identified by their texture and often by their excellent wool.*

*Figure 46. Quchan Kurd rug from Khurasan. These rugs with geometric figures are often unusually thick. Although the Quchan Kurds in the east and the Kurds in western Iran have been separated for several hundred years, there are still many common design elements in the two types of rug. This suggests that the Kurds were weaving rugs well before one part of the population was settled on Persia's eastern border.*

*Figure 47 (opposite). Mid-nineteenth century Hamadan rug in a traditional design. During the first half of the twentieth century there were probably more rugs from the Hamadan area exported to the West than any other type. Most were small, and the range of designs was enormous.*

A group of Kurds that were transplanted to an area in eastern Iran near the town of Quchan have continued to weave rugs, although they have evolved in different directions during the last several centuries **(Figure 46)**. Some Quchan Kurd rugs are woven in designs adapted from the Turkmen, and another group has taken on Baluchi features, although the symmetrical knot has been retained. Although they were separated from the western Kurds in the seventeenth century, it is interesting to see that some of the rugs still show designs essentially identical to those of the western Kurds.

*Hamadan*

The Hamadan area has probably supplied more rugs to the West during the last century than any other part of Iran, although they are generally of rather coarse weave with generic Persian patterns. They are not made within the city of Hamadan itself, but in several hundred villages in the surrounding area. These rugs almost exclusively employ a structure that sets them apart from most other symmetrically knotted village rugs. They have only one weft between the rows of knots, and this may easily be seen from inspecting the back of the rug. Only the Bakhtiari types of the Chahar Mahal and a few rugs from the Heriz district have this characteristic. Very early Hamadans may have a wool foundation, but almost all examples from the last century have cotton **(Figure 47)**.

Although the designs are taken from the standard Persian repertoire, with many pieces woven in crude variants of the herati or mina khani patterns, they show a wide range of variation on common motifs. A number of the rugs show botehs of different sizes, while others have repeating geometric figures. Most are in small sizes or in a runner format, and only a few places in the Hamadan district weave large rugs.

Two parts of the district weave a finer than average grade than the typical Hamadan. The Malayer area produces a rug that is fine enough at times to be mistaken for a Senneh, which it often resembles in design. The Jozan area

*Figure 48. Jozan medallion rug of the late nineteenth century. While the designs resemble those of Sarouk rugs, the Jozan is symmetrically knotted and often shows more abrash.*

produces a finer symmetrically knotted rug that often resembles the earlier Sarouk in design, with which it also shares the use of two wefts between the rows of knots. Jozan rugs are often more heavily abrashed than the Sarouk (**Figure 48**).

The earliest generation of Hamadans to reach the West often had a camel-coloured field, and many of them were in a runner format. While these pieces are often described as woven of camel hair, this is not the case, as the wool has simply been dyed in a tan colour, often with walnut husks or gall nuts.

*Heriz*

Heriz is the centre of a cluster of towns and villages to the east of Tabriz, where a popular type of medallion rug is woven. It is thick, coarsely knotted, and has been relatively inexpensive (**Figure 49**). Few surviving examples are found in anything but larger sizes, from about 8 x 10 and 9 x 12 feet (2.4 x 3 and 2.75 x 3.65 metres) up to much larger examples. While Hamadan supplied scatter sizes in the early twentieth century, the Heriz area was the major supplier of relatively inexpensive room-sized carpets.

*Figure 49. Heriz rug from the late nineteenth century of a type that was exported, with little change in design, over a period of many decades. These were probably originally based upon the typical Persian city medallion rug, except that the relatively coarse weave has made the design less curvilinear.*

Those with natural dyes that have survived in good condition, however, have become extremely expensive, although reproductions of Heriz rugs with natural dyes have recently become common.

The rugs are symmetrically knotted and labelled not so much by place of origin, but by grade, although the grades are based upon village names. For the last century the finest grade has been described as a Serapi, often with designs verging on the curvilinear. Finely woven rugs, now described as Ahar, are also somewhat curvilinear and may show an unusual feature in which many of the stylised floral figures may be outlined in two colours rather than the usual single outline. The term Gorevan was formerly used for the lower grades, but it is less used now, and many are labelled simply as Heriz.

While most of the rugs have medallion designs, perhaps 10 per cent have overall designs of large stylised floral and leaf forms. For some reason the classic herati and boteh designs so common from other parts of Iran were seldom used in this area.

Most of the rugs have two wefts between the rows

Figure 50. During the nineteenth century there was a small production of finely woven silk rugs from the Tabriz/Heriz area. This type is usually labelled as a silk Heriz, although there is a strong possibility that all such silk rugs were woven in Tabriz. Approx. 70½ x 53½ins. (179 x 136cm).

Figure 51 (opposite). Bakhtiari rug in the most common design in which the field is divided into square compartments filled with stylised floral figures. This rendition of the design may date from the last part of the nineteenth century, as more recent versions show a repetition of the same motifs with a darker colour scheme.

of knots, but several villages use only one weft between the rows, including the town of Karadja, which is known for long narrow rugs. These rugs are generally attractive and durable. Colours early in the century were excellent, but later periods featured less attractive synthetic colours.

The town of Sarab in the southern part of the Heriz district is known for its long rugs with a limited range of designs on a camel-coloured field.

A group of silk rugs from the late nineteenth century are often given the label of Heriz, although most may have been woven within Tabriz (**Figure 50**).

*The Chahar Mahal*

A group of villages in the Zagros foothills just west of Isfahan comprises a weaving area whose rugs are often labelled as Bakhtiari, although many weavers are Kurdish villagers. The rugs resemble the Hamadan in structure, with the use of only one weft between the rows of knots, but generally have darker colours, with more brown and dark green. Many examples are found with squarish or lozenge-shaped compartments within which are found stylised floral figures (**Figure 51**). These rugs are thick and come in a wide range of sizes. The Bakhtiari also weave

*Figure 52. Although the gabbeh rugs of Persia show simple designs, small structural features at times allow them to be identified as to tribal source. This was woven by the Bakhtiari, although it contains no specific tribal features. Approx. 108 x 56½ins. (274 x 144cm).*

### Other towns of note

The town of Joshaqan, south of Kashan, has a long tradition of making carpets. The rugs are of medium grade, asymmetrically knotted on a cotton foundation, and are characterised by designs with stylised floral sprays configured in a lozenge shape, at times with a small medallion. There has been little change in the traditional designs for over a century (**Figure 53**). Several other nearby towns have taken to weaving the classic design, some in a tighter weave. Occasionally one will find a rug in a Bakhtiari weave and a Joshaqan design.

### Lilihan

Although the Lilihan rug is woven in a number of villages, it resembles city rugs from the Arak region. During the mid-twentieth century rugs for the American market were woven here, often with dark maroon field colours and a design of detached floral sprays similar to the contemporary Sarouk The structure is distinctive in that the rugs are made with asymmetrical knots, but there is usually only one weft between the rows of knots. Most single wefted rugs are symmetrically knotted.

## RUGS OF THE IRANIAN NOMADS

While the Iranian government, for much of the twentieth century, attempted to settle its population of nomads, there are a number of tribes still practising at least partial nomadism. This involves part of the tribe migrating to progressively higher ground in the spring and summer to find fresh pasturage for their flocks, and then returning to the lowlands for the cold season. Parts of each tribe remain sedentary, growing cereal crops for survival over the winter. Eventually this way of life

gabbeh rugs, a thick, coarse, symmetrically knotted fabric with simple geometric designs, and a wide variety of nomadic trappings (**Figure 52**).

Recent Bakhtiari rugs have a cotton foundation, although there are surviving examples from an earlier generation woven on wool warps and wefts.

*Figure 53. Rugs from the town of Joshaqan in central Iran have maintained the same design – with variations – for well over a century. Some of them show a fine enough weave to be classified among the city rugs.*

will probably become extinct, as migrating nomads have always been problematic for governments. Nomads have been difficult to control, and their lifestyle has led to a certain independence from central authority. It also has led to rugs with a different visual flavour from those of the Persian villagers, and consequently nomadic rugs have held a special appeal for the collector.

The large city of Shiraz in southern Iran is not a significant producer of rugs, but there are many weavers among the nomadic and village populations of the surrounding areas. In addition to the villagers, who are mostly of indigenous Iranian stock, there are two major tribal groups with their own leadership structures: the Qashqa'i and the Khamseh Federation.

Year after year these groups have moved their flocks from the lowlands to higher ground as the summer progresses, and these moves have developed a certain complexity in which the same transit areas are often occupied by different tribes at different stages in their migrations. Then as the weather cools, and the tribes move toward their winter quarters, the same pattern of movement takes place. Over the centuries alliances and enmities have developed between the different tribal groups, and no doubt at times in the past there has been open conflict.

### The Qashqa'i

The Qashqa'i, a grouping mostly of Turkic origin, and the dominant tribe of the region, is made up of a number of subtribes including the Qashguli, Bulli, Darashuri, Kuhi, and others. There are theories that the first of these Turkic people entered the Fars region in the thirteenth century, having been forced south by the arrival of Mongol armies in Azerbaijan. At times the Qashqa'i have represented a powerful force within Persia, as a migrating tribe is organised along military lines, with all men essentially able to function as warriors. There has also always been a certain friction, and interdependence, between the migratory and settled populations.

The Qashqa'i weave two types of rugs. Probably the most ancient tradition is the gabbeh rug. These have probably been woven for local use for centuries, and until recently have been ignored by collectors.

The rugs most frequently woven for the market are all of wool, asymmetrically knotted and are based primarily upon traditional Persian designs, with frequent use of the herati pattern, at times with a small medallion. The repeating boteh also occurs on many Qashqa'i rugs, and adaptations of the Moghul *mille fleurs* design in a prayer rug format are also woven, but these are ordinarily made in the workshops of settled tribespeople around the town of Firuzabad rather than by nomads.

*Figure 54. Qashqa'i rug, probably from the Qashguli subtribe, with repeating boteh figures. Distinguishing Qashqa'i rugs from those of the Khamseh is often difficult, but the former usually have ivory warps, and the wefts are more likely to be dyed red. It is rare to find a symmetrically knotted Qashqa'i except among the gabbehs. Approx. 72½ x 53ins. (184 x 134cm).*

*Figure 55. Qashqa'i rug with a characteristic small medallion and a blue field with a variety of repeating figures. Assigning a Qashqa'i rug to a specific subtribe is based more upon the fineness of weave than upon the design elements, which are shared among the various groups.*

Qashqa'i rugs often show a variety of ornaments arranged with less formality than one would find on a Persian city rug, and they carry about them a liveliness often lacking in the typical village rug. Many nomadic rug enthusiasts see these pieces as adhering more to earlier and non-commercial traditions than the rugs of settled people, and yet that may be an exaggeration. The degree to which these rugs predate the expansion of the Persian rug industry in the late nineteenth century is still not clear, although a few have inwoven dates suggesting a mid-century origin. This brings up the question of whether the original Qashqa'i products are the gabbehs and kilims, while the asymmetrically knotted rugs in non-tribal designs may represent a later commercial production.

The best of these rugs are powerfully coloured and boldly designed, often showing additional simple geometric border stripes at both ends (**Figures 54 and 55**). There has never been a large supply of the higher grade Qashqa'i rugs, and the best are avidly sought by collectors.

A number of trappings associated with nomadic life

*Figure 56. Gabbeh rug, all wool, with crudely drawn animal figures. While these are now commercial items, they were formerly woven for local use. Although this is almost certainly Qashqa'i work, gabbehs are difficult to assign to a specific tribal group.*

are also made by the Qashqa'i, including many kilims, horse covers, and a number of bags. Qashqa'i kilims in particular are woven in vivid colours that resemble more the gabbehs than the other Qashqa'i pile weaves **(Figure 56)**.

### The Khamseh Federation

This is a grouping of tribes of diverse origins, including Arabs, native Iranian tribes such as the Lors, and Turkic groups not allied with the Qashqa'i. The Arab tribe includes a number of Arabic speaking peoples, some of whom claim to have migrated into Iran from the Arabian Peninsula at the time of the Islamic conquest in the seventh century. Turkic elements are found among the Baharlu and Ainalu, while a number of tribes have members of Lor descent. Not surprisingly rugs of these peoples cover a range of types, although they are often difficult to distinguish

from each other and at times may resemble Qashqa'i rugs. One characteristic is that Khamseh rugs are more likely to show dark wool warps, while warps of Qashqa'i rugs are more commonly ivory. Khamseh rugs are also not so likely to be double-warped and are generally looser in construction.

Earlier pieces may show great charm and excellent colours, although the colour scheme is often slightly more subdued than that found on Qashqa'i rugs. One often encounters a design in which stylised bird figures are repeated in different colours throughout the field **(Figure 57)**. There are some examples with three or more simple, lozenge-shaped medallions along the vertical axis **(Figure 58)**. The rugs are variable in size, but seldom exceed about 6 x 12 feet (1.82 x 3.65 metres). Prayer rug designs are rare, but there are a few pictorial rugs. Often one finds repeating geometric figures with relatively narrow borders.

*Figure 57. Khamseh rug with an allover pattern of birds. This is a common design on Khamseh rugs and may be a product of the Arab subtribe. Such rugs are less likely to be double-warped than Qashga'i rugs and consequently have a looser feel to them.*

*Figure 58. Khamseh rug in a typical pattern with three small lozenge-shaped medallions on a field of small repeating figures. The same format is often found on Qashga'i rugs, although they include a different range of subsidiary figures.*

63

*Figure 59 (opposite). Lori rug with a dark tonality common to this group. These are usually less finely woven than Qashqa'i rugs, and the Lori use a variety of designs common to the Shiraz area.*

*Figure 60. Gabbeh rug in strong primary colours woven by the Lori tribe. The exact tribal origin could be argued in this case, but the strong primary colours are suggestive of a Lori group.*

Some rugs are identifiable as products of various Lori tribes, some of whom are affiliated with the Khamseh (**Figure 59**). There are also some particularly colourful Lori gabbeh rugs which are difficult to distinguish from those of the Qashqa'i (**Figure 60**).

The Khamseh Federation does not have the same kinds of historic traditions as the Qashqa'i, as it was formed only in the nineteenth century. Primarily it was assembled by external political forces attempting to form something of a counterweight to the powerful Qashqa'i. As the Khamseh Federation is made up of disparate elements, it has not maintained the same political clout as the Qashqa'i, and it appears to be diminishing in importance.

### Gabbeh rugs from the Shiraz area

In the late 1980s the Shiraz area was the centre of the natural dyeing revival that has had a great impact on the entire rug industry within Iran. As natural dyeing had essentially completely disappeared from Iran, it took several enterprising dyers to began experimenting with such materials as madder, natural indigo, and yellow dyes from native plants. For reasons not entirely clear, many of the earliest rugs from this project were gabbehs, with a relatively coarse weave and bold, simple designs.

When these appeared at a major trade fair in Tehran in 1992, the results left a deep impact on many of the dealers in attendance, but there were still some needed

adjustments. The reds seemed a little too sombre, and the yellows appeared to be the wrong quality. Within several years, however, the necessary adjustments had been made, and the naturally dyed gabbeh became a great commercial success. The gabbeh was originally associated with the nomadic way of life, while the new production is clearly a commercial enterprise. As these gabbeh do not represent tribal rugs, the new production cannot be identified as either Qashqa'i or Khamseh, and has become more of a regional enterprise. It has also been widely copied abroad, and one now finds Shiraz-type gabbeh rugs from Pakistan and India.

## The Afshar

While village and nomadic rugs from rural parts of the province of Kerman are often described as products of the Afshar, there are a number of peoples living in this area, although weavings of specific groups are extremely difficult to distinguish. Those with symmetrical knots are said to have been woven by nomads of Turkic origin, while asymmetrically knotted rugs are attributed to villagers of Iranian descent, although no doubt there are exceptions. The rugs are usually small, although there are a small number of nineteenth century pieces made in adaptations of city designs.

The old rugs are all wool, while more recent examples have a cotton foundation. Some pieces have long flatwoven bands at both ends, as one finds on some Turkmen rugs. Many of the designs show stylised versions of city designs, with stiff medallions or botehs (**Figures 61 and 62**). Some show repeating geometric figures. Field colour is often of blue, and many of the rugs show as much blue as red. A large number of bags are found from this area, as are flatweaves in a variety of structures.

*Figure 61 (opposite). Afshar rug in a medallion design. Note the stylised vases and flowers, which suggest that the design is an adaptation from a city rug in which the vase and flowers would be realistically drawn.*

*Figure 62 (left). Afshar rug with a repeating boteh design on an ivory field. The boteh is a common device among the various groups making rugs labelled as Afshar. It varies from a small figure less than 2ins. (5cm) in size to large figures of over 12ins. (30.5cm). At times the large boteh figures show small botehs within.*

*Figure 63. Baluchi rugs often appear only in dark tones, but this bag face has strong highlights in ivory. The figures in the field often include birds or other repeating devices, and occasionally the finest of these pieces will show patches of silk pile.*

### The Baluchi

The Baluchi live in eastern Iran, adjoining parts of western Afghanistan, as well as parts of Pakistan. They speak an Indo-Iranian language, and ordinarily inhabit the poorest parts of the three countries, living on their flocks of sheep and with probably a smaller settled component than either the nomads of the Shiraz or Kerman areas.

Baluchi rugs are the darkest group of Near Eastern pileweaves. They are asymmetrically knotted on a wool foundation and, except for a group of Baluchi rugs from north-western Afghanistan, are usually small. Rugs of the nomadic Baluchi usually show a three or four bundle selvage of dark goat hair on the sides and kilim ends that may be decorated with rows of weft float or other flatweave technique.

There are many Baluchi saddlebags, often larger than most found elsewhere, and the designs may consist of repeated geometric figures or stiffly-drawn bird figures. At some point there is usually a figure in ivory which stands out from darker colours (**Figure 63**). Pieces with prayer rug designs are common, usually with a squared mihrab and often showing a tree-of-life design or repeated geometric figures. Baluchi rugs woven in and around the Iranian towns of Turbat-i-Heydari and Turbat-i-Jam are finer than most others, and often show renditions of the herati or mina khani design (**Figures 64 and 65**).

*Figure 64. Baluchi-type rug made by the Taimani of Afghanistan. The Taimani are not a Baluchi tribe, but have been weaving rugs in the same dark tones and simple geometric designs. Taimani rugs, however, are less likely to show flatwoven stripes with designs at both ends.*

*Figure 65. Baluchi rugs from the area south and east of Mashhad are among the most finely woven of the type, and often show adaptations of such classic Persian designs as the herati and mina khani.*

Until the last part of the twentieth century Baluchi rugs were among the least expensive hand-knotted floor coverings, and they were often regarded as beneath the notice of the serious collector. This has dramatically changed, as a number of serious collections based on Baluchi rugs have been formed, and a wide literature on the type has accumulated. What was formerly seen as small, sombre, loosely woven rugs, are now taken seriously, backed up as they are with a careful analysis of designs and iconography.

*The Shahsevan and rugs of the Veramin area*
The Shahsevan are a nomadic and semi-nomadic group scattered about eastern Azerbaijan, with some migrating as far south as the Hamadan Plain in winter. In the summer their pasturage is farther north, mostly on the Savalan Massif east of Tabriz. Their best known woven products are attractive bags in a fine soumak structure, although one may find less distinguished pile rugs in north Persian bazaars that

are described as Shahsevan work. From time to time, finely woven kilims are attributed to the Shahsevan, although the label at times seems to be assigned without hard information on origin.

While there are some city-type rugs woven in Veramin, usually in the mina khani design, rugs with this label are often woven by nomadic groups who winter in the area around the city because of its relatively mild weather. These tribes include some Shahsevan, Lori, Kurds, and other groups, whose woven products includes a number of bags, animal trappings, and a type of kilim in 'eye dazzler' designs, with a vivid interaction of strong colours (**Figure 66**). At times the Veramin label seems to be loosely applied to small tribal pieces which cannot be more specifically identified.

*Turkmen nomads*
The rugs of Turkmen nomads from the north-eastern part of Iran will be described in Chapter 6, which includes descriptions of rugs from Turkmenistan.

*Figure 66. Kilim possibly woven by the Shahsevan of north-western Iran. As one would expect, the designs are rigidly geometric, and the colours boldly contrasting. While the exact local origin of such a piece cannot be determined, it seems to belong within the cultural sphere of Azerbaijan, although one cannot be certain on which side of the national borders it was woven. Approx. 94 x 69ins. (239 x 176cm).*

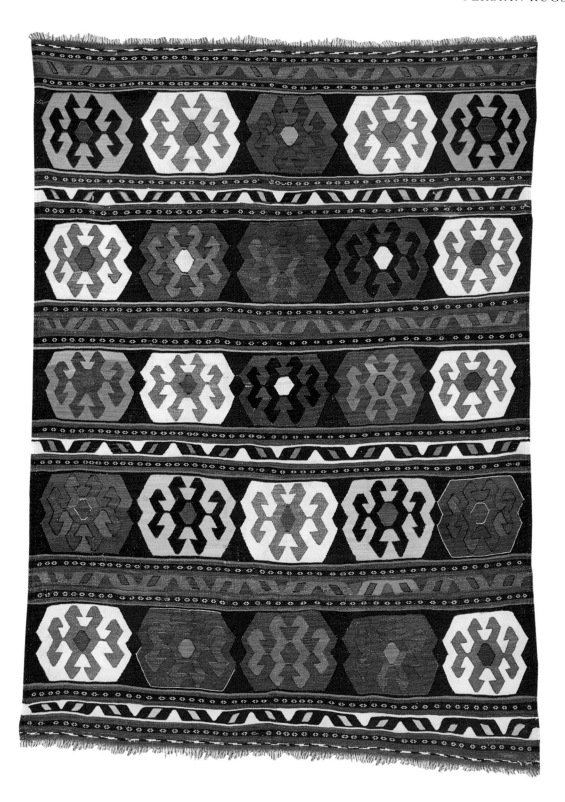

# CHAPTER 4

# TURKISH RUGS

Rugs were almost certainly made in the area of modern Turkey well before the Turks began arriving in the second half of the first millennium A.D., but their conquest of Asia Minor changed its alignment from the Greek/Byzantine world and allied it with the Islamic Near East. Knotted pile carpets survive from the fourteenth century and quite possibly a century or two earlier; the earliest are to be found in major museums. What must have been a brisk trade in rugs with Europe began early, as rugs from Anatolia began to appear as decorative items in Italian Renaissance paintings of the thirteenth century, and many surviving pieces have been found in Europe, particularly in Italy, for the Venetians and Genoese were long the major traders between the Ottoman Empire and Europe.

While there has been a relatively small rug industry in Istanbul during the last centuries, though several cities in the middle part of the country have also produced rugs, there has been much less of a tradition of city rugs in Turkey than in Iran. The nomads of Anatolia have not been so powerful in relation to the Ottoman state as the most important nomadic groups have been in Iran, and it is probable they have not been the major producers of rugs, although they have been responsible for a large number of kilims.

## DEVELOPMENT OF THE TURKISH RUG

What are generally thought to be the earliest Turkish rugs of which any records survive are to be found in paintings of the early Italian Renaissance when, in the thirteenth century, a number of carpets begin to appear in both religious and secular paintings. They may be found under the chair in which the Madonna sits, or perhaps draped over a windowsill or even on a floor on which people are standing. While there is no way of knowing for certain that the models for these painted rugs came from Turkey, by the fourteenth century some of them show bird and animal forms similar to those that appear on the few surviving Turkish pieces, probably from the fourteenth century. These pieces are structurally enough like later rugs

known to be Turkish that most carpet scholars believe them to be Turkish work.

Yet there are problems with this hypothesis. There is some reason to believe that carpets were woven in parts of the Byzantine world – and one cannot even rule out the possibility that early animal carpets began to be woven – before the Turks came to dominate western Anatolia. There is also a question as to which Turkic group wove them, as a group of carpets found in a thirteenth century mosque in Konya – usually attributed to the Seljuks – do not at all resemble the animal carpets. Furthermore, the Ottomans appear to have been more fundamentalist in their approach to Islam and did not include animal figures on their rugs. There have even been suggestions that the rugs depicted in Italian paintings may have been woven in Italy.

By the fifteenth century, however, a group of carpets named after the European painter Hans Holbein – whose paintings showed a number of examples – are clearly attributable to the Ottomans.

There are small pattern Holbeins and large pattern Holbeins, and – as if to complicate the question of where the designs originated – both types also have surviving nearly identical counterparts from Spain. The Turkish versions are generally assumed to be the earliest, but this is by no means an established fact.

By the sixteenth century, a number of new Turkish types of rugs appeared, and these survive in greater numbers so that examples are still occasionally found on the market, while the previously mentioned earlier pieces are almost all in museum collections. Prominent among this new type of rug is a complex design named for the Venetian painter Lorenzo Lotto, who depicted several. There are also Spanish versions of Lotto rugs.

An important production from an identifiable location seems to have begun in the fifteenth century, and in the following centuries appears to have been responsible for an enormous number of rugs, many of which have survived. The area around the town of Ushak in western Anatolia became a rug centre of great importance, possibly beginning with the Holbein and

*Figure 67. Turkish rug from the Aegean region woven in the vicinity of Çanakkale and Ezine, with two medallions. These rugs seem to represent a long tradition in this region, as examples with similar designs can be found over a period of at least two hundred years and possibly much longer.*

many museum collections. They were a successful commercial product, with a worldwide trade that made them sought as far afield as sixteenth century England.

Probably at about the same time as the production from Ushak appeared, another type of rug, associated with the Ottoman court, was woven. While these are often considered to be later than the Ushak pieces, the two types – of enormously different textures – share some features of design. These court rugs are asymmetrically knotted, often have silk warps, and show high knot counts. At times there are highlights of blue or white cotton. The features that make them unusual are their asymmetrical knotting and use of S-spun yarns, both features associated with Egyptian weaving, and there is some possibility that the Ottoman court carpets were woven in Cairo.

While there are still many questions of chronology and design origins, it is clear that rugs woven throughout Turkey since the sixteenth century often show design features that are descended from the early Ushak production or that associated with the Ottoman court. While the Turkish rug of the nineteenth and twentieth centuries, as it is appreciated by the collector, is primarily a village product, many features are directly descended from earlier court rugs or the enormous output of the Ushak looms. There are literally hundreds of rug weaving villages through Anatolia, and a regional approach, mentioning only the most significant villages and towns, is followed here. As a rule these rugs are all symmetrically knotted and, except where noted, are all of wool.

**THE AEGEAN REGION**

The most north-western part of Anatolia has probably produced rugs since at least the fourteenth century, if not earlier in Byzantine times. The most common labels are Çanakkale and Ezine, the two major population centres, although most of the rugs are produced in smaller villages. They are relatively coarsely knotted, seldom reaching 50 knots per square inch, although they characteristically have strong colours, with excellent reds, somewhat less blue, and more ivory than is seen in most other Anatolian types. Designs are bold and have a superficial resemblance to rugs of the Caucasus (**Figure 67**). Some of the

Lotto types, but certainly involved in the production of types described as the medallion Ushak and the star Ushak. Both were based on endless repeats of two different figures, usually with the subsidiary figures bisected by the borders. Hundreds of medallion Ushaks survive in sizes often exceeding 20 feet (6.1 metres). The earlier pieces are finer in weave than later examples, and the reds appear to be more saturated in them. The star Ushak is usually smaller in size and more finely woven. There are a number of other designs, usually of large stylised floral figures.

Most of the large pre-twentieth century rugs from Anatolia were probably woven in Ushak. The medallion and star design rugs from Ushak are to be found in

*Figure 68. Turkish rug from the Aegean region. Clearly this design is a descendant of the large pattern Holbein-type that first appeared as early as the fifteenth century.*

*Figure 69 (above left). This rug was woven in western Turkey in an area north of Bergama. The subdued colours are typical of the region, and the type has no doubt been woven over a period of at least several centuries.*

*Figure 70 (above right). Rug from the Bergama area with typical border stripes and a colour tonality built around red, blue, and ivory. For the last century a large number of small rugs, flat-woven bags, and kilims have originated from the Bergama district. The ruins of an ancient Greek city nearby raise questions about the age of the weaving tradition in this region.*

designs can be traced back hundreds of years, in particular the large pattern Holbein-type appear to have descendants in this area (**Figure 68**).

*Bergama and its environs*
Bergama was an important city in Greek and Roman times, and the region maintained a large Greek population until the 1920s. Rugs from the Bergama region are often given the label Yağcibedir, after a tribal group in the area that was once nomadic. Many

of the pile rugs of the region are rather sombre in colour, with strong blues and reds, and some ivory highlights (**Figures 69 and 70**). Earlier Bergamas show a livelier colour scheme, with more apricot, green, and yellow. Another group shows paler colours in earth tones. The rugs are usually small, often in a prayer rug format, and at times the field is composed on a large lozenge with stylised flowers.

Many flatwoven bags and kilims, usually small, are woven in the Bergama area.

## THE USHAK AREA

As noted above, Ushak was not only important in early rug production, but has continued through the twentieth century to produce carpets (**Figure 71**). These have included the revival of earlier patterns, as well as newer types with pastel colours and thick piles. Some of these rugs are still very large, with thick, shaggy pile. Nineteenth century rugs from this region were extremely coarse, and the colours usually pale. A large thick type of prayer rug was among the later examples from this town.

*Gördes*

Not far from Ushak is the town of Gördes (Ghiordes in older rug literature). Prayer rugs from this area were among the most avidly sought types during the first quarter of the twentieth century. The rugs were notable for elaborate designs, complex borders of geo-metrised flowers, and cross panels usually above and below the mihrab. Colours, usually based around an ivory, red, or blue field, were often especially harmonious. The field frequently showed a hanging lamp, at times with columns along the sides (**Figure 72**). In the late nineteenth century a number of rugs were woven here with European designs. Because they are associated with styles favoured by the Sultan Abd ul- Mejid, they are often called Mejedieh rugs.

Structurally, later Gördes rugs often show cotton wefts and cotton for areas of white pile. Earlier pieces had wool wefts and used madder reds, while later pieces used cochineal for red shades.

*Figure 71 (above). The town of Ushak has woven rugs on a commercial basis since at least the fifteenth century. Medallion rugs of this type are some of the most frequently found rugs dating to the seventeenth century or earlier. The corners show parts of a medallion that differs greatly from the central medallion. At times more or less of these secondary medallions appear, while occasionally there are two or even three of the main medallions. These rugs can reach over 30 feet (9 metres) in length.*

*Figure 72 (opposite). Gördes prayer rug, probably eighteenth century. The designs were based upon earlier Ottoman court rugs, with columns and cross panels. The hanging lamp from the top of the mihrab is a variable feature. In later rugs the field becomes progressively smaller.*

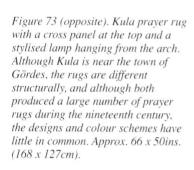

*Figure 73 (opposite). Kula prayer rug with a cross panel at the top and a stylised lamp hanging from the arch. Although Kula is near the town of Gördes, the rugs are different structurally, and although both produced a large number of prayer rugs during the nineteenth century, the designs and colour schemes have little in common. Approx. 66 x 50ins. (168 x 127cm).*

*Figure 74. Kula rug with niches at each end of the field. The muted earth tones are characteristic of the type. The colour scheme here is typical of late nineteenth century Kulas, with an emphasis on earth tones.*

## Kula

The town of Kula, near Gördes, also produced a much admired prayer rug from the eighteenth century and possibly earlier. The Kula usually was a longer narrower rug, with cross panels only at the top and more austere earth tones of rust red, yellows, and relatively little blue (**Figures 73 and 74**), although there are both blue and red field prayer rugs. The borders were simpler than on the Gördes, and there is no use of cotton in either weft or pile. The knotting is less fine than on the Gördes, although the structure is particularly tough.

During the last several decades the Kula area has often produced commercial rugs featuring designs copied from other areas. Caucasian designs have been woven here, in an undistinguished range of rather dull colours.

*Selindi*

A number of ivory field rugs are attributed to the town of Selindi, which is part of the region including Kula and Gördes. Some examples may date to the seventeenth century, including pieces with the so-called Chintamanni and bird designs. Later white field rugs of this sort are often given the Gördes label, since they show the same use of cotton wefts and areas of ivory pile **(Figure 75)**.

*Demirci*

The town of Demirci has also produced an identifiable type of rug that has shown a slow evolution over the last several hundred year **(Figure 76)**. Many are dark, and there are often structural peculiarities with an occasional use of single wefts between the rows of knots. The designs show similarities to many of the so-called Transylvania rugs, although they are quite different in colour. Often these rugs are labelled as a type of Kula.

## THE SOUTH-WEST ANATOLIAN COAST

While a number of towns and villages in this area weave rugs, most are labelled as Milas or Makri, the latter term applying to rugs from the area around Fethiye. Nineteenth century examples of both types are sought by collectors.

The Milas usually appears in two design forms. The typical prayer rug has a mihrab with indentations toward the upper portion creating a lozenge-shaped area. There is usually an ivory field in the area above the mihrab, with stylised floral figures, and there may be a stylised hanging lamp. The red is often a rather pale rust colour, while the border usually shows a deep yellow field. Green and mauve are used sparingly. The less commonly encountered stripe Milas design involves panels running the length of the rug, and there may or may not be a niche at one end. This type may be associated with the nearby town of Karaova rather than Milas itself **(Figure 77)**.

*Figure 75 (opposite left). Although white field rugs of this type have often been attributed to Gördes, they are now thought to have been woven in the nearby town of Selindi. The wefts are usually cotton, and the ivory part of the pile is also usually knotted in cotton. Approx. 116½ x 48½ins. (148 x 123cm).*

*Figure 76 (opposite right). Demirci rug with a design of stylised floral figures. This is a particularly early example, with a design that evolved over a period of well over a century. Later examples of the type are unusually dark for a Turkish rug.*

*Figure 77. Stripe Milas rug with colours often associated with the south-western area of Turkey. Although the format of this rug appears on many rugs from the Milas area, there is surprising variability in the colours and design details. Approx. 59½ x 37½ins. (151 x 95cm).*

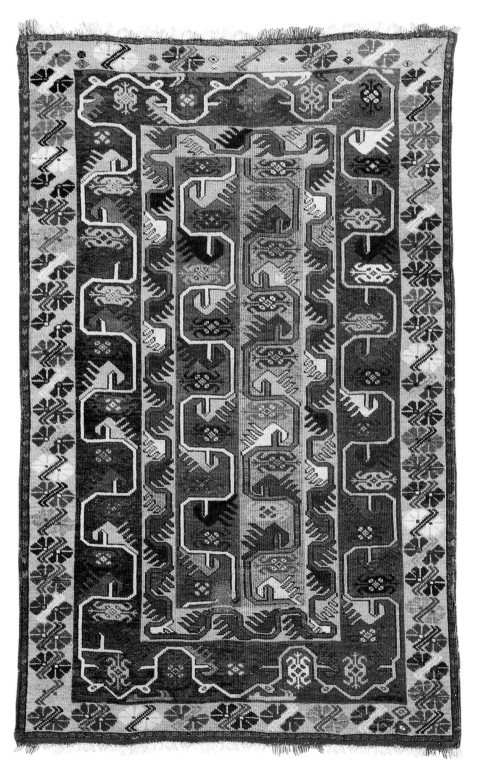

The Makri is usually found in prayer rug designs, with one, two, or three longitudinal panels. The rugs are woven with more blue, often in lighter shades, than the typical Milas, and the reds often tend toward the brownish; yellow and ivory may be prominent (**Figure 78**). The Makri are generally thicker and less finely woven than the Milas.

From the southern coast of Anatolia slightly inland from Antalya, rugs are woven around the town of Dosmealti. These usually show repeating designs on a dark field, with an unusual prominence of green. The type may be traced back to the eighteenth century.

## RUGS OF CENTRAL ANATOLIA

Although there are many rug weaving villages in central Turkey, it is possible to generalise about the majority of them. The rugs are usually lighter in overall tone than western Anatolian rugs, and they average a slightly lower knot count. Konya is the primary market for central Anatolian rugs, and consequently a large number of diverse pieces are often sold under this label. They are usually of medium fineness, but occasionally coarse. There is seldom a really strong red, but often the field in both prayer rugs and runners is some shade of yellow (**Figure 79**). There is a type of long rug with a

*Figure 78 (opposite left). Makri prayer rug with a single niche. There are also examples with two and three niches. Most rugs of the region appear in prayer rug designs and are often characterised by an unusual amount of light blue rather than the reddish tonality so common on the Milas-type rugs made in an adjacent region. Approx. 64½ x 41ins. (164 x 104cm).*

*Figure 79 (opposite right). Classic prayer rug from the Konya region with columns based on earlier Ottoman designs. The colour scheme on this example is classic for the type, with clear earth tones. The rugs are generally of a rather loose weave. Approx. 61½ x 42½ins. (156 x 108cm).*

*Figure 80. Long rug from the Konya area with classic eight-pointed stars within square compartments. Long rugs of this general type were woven in dozens of villages in the Konya area, with many showing a prominent use of a deep yellow and many subsidiary colours.*

yellow field and often two rows of geometric motifs, including one often described as a Memling gul, after the painter Hans Memling, who depicted one in a fifteenth century painting.

There is a squarish type of Konya rug known as a yatak that was often used as a sleeping rug. These are particularly thick and are usually decorated with rows of geometric figures and a narrow border. Many small pillow covers, called yastiks, have been woven around Konya, as have many long rugs (**Figure 80**).

*Figure 81. Ladik prayer rug with an unusual narrow field and the cross panel above the arch. Examples of this sort are more often dated than most Turkish rugs, and some can clearly be attributed to the eighteenth century. The type seems descended from Ottoman court rugs, as some show columns, and most have cross panels with large tulip plants.*

## Ladik

The Ladik prayer rug, from a town to the north and west of Konya, was of prime interest to collectors during the first half of the twentieth century. They are readily recognisable, with a single long cross panel of stylised tulips. This panel may cross above or below the mihrab, which is usually stepped, and the field beneath the mihrab may be open – as on some rugs thought to be earlier – or filled with large geometric figures probably representing stylised lamps, with geometric figures in the spandrels. There are several characteristic borders. Occasionally one finds a Ladik with an inwoven date. The colours are often intense, with strong reds set against medium blue, at times with yellow highlights **(Figure 81)**.

## Kirshehir and Mucur

Among the many types of central Anatolian rugs sought by collectors are the prayer rugs of Kirshehir

*Figure 82 (opposite right). Kirshehir prayer rug in a typical format. These rugs are often unusual in the number of different colours used. The field is usually red, but blue, green, and ivory fields are also known. The range of border stripes is small.*

*Figure 83. Mucur prayer rug with a cross panel above the arch. Like the Kirshehir, rugs from the nearby town of Mucur include a wide range of colours, and the designs are similar. A red field is also most common here. Approx. 65 x 48ins. (165 x 122cm).*

and Mucur, two nearby towns whose weaves bear a strong resemblance to one another (**Figures 82 and 83**). The prayer rugs are particularly notable, usually with a red or green field, rarely ivory. There are often more than a dozen distinct colours, which is rare for an Anatolian rug. Madder was used in the earlier pieces, but during the late nineteenth century cochineal became more common for the reds. Although there is no structural way to tell which rugs are from Kirshehir and which from Mucur, there is a particular border associated with Mucur.

A small number of long rugs were woven in this area, and some Mejedieh types were woven here during the late nineteenth century.

### Kayseri

The city of Kayseri has long been a source of commercial rugs rather than Turkish village rugs, and the designs have often involved adaptations from other areas. While rugs have probably been woven in this area for many centuries, one seldom sees a surviving Kayseri rug that is likely to predate the late nineteenth century. Those rugs woven within the city almost all have a cotton foundation, and the designs may even include adaptations of Persian medallion rugs. A number of prayer rug adaptations have been woven in Kayseri, usually of types related to Ottoman court prayer rugs or early Gördes types. Usually these adaptations are slightly to substantially smaller than the originals, and many are woven with a mercerised cotton pile and foundation. Mercerised cotton has a silk-like lustre, and the rugs are often sold as silk or 'Turkish silk', a euphemism for mercerised cotton. Saffs in mercerised cotton are also frequently encountered.

### Sivas

The city of Sivas, north-east of Kayseri, has also focused upon commercial rugs with cotton foundations. Early in the twentieth century a series of pictorial rugs was woven here, usually in attenuated colours, and adaptations of Persian designs are also woven. Rugs from the surrounding countryside, however, are strictly of the village or nomadic type, relating to an entirely different tradition from the city rugs.

## RUGS FROM EASTERN ANATOLIA

Although the rugs of eastern Anatolia, like other Turkish rugs, are woven with the symmetrical knot

*Figure 84 (opposite left). Turkish nomadic rug in a design that has been associated with several nomadic groups. It is easier to identify the area where a rug was made when recent examples with the same designs are found on the market. Yet there are so many eastern Turkish villages still weaving rugs that at times it is difficult to be certain of a rug's origin.*

*Figure 85 (opposite right). Eastern Anatolian rug of a type now usually labelled as Kagizman. Like several other types from this area, rugs in this design were woven over a period of perhaps two centuries, as examples survive suggesting considerable age. Approx. 83½ x 45ins. (212 x 114cm).*

*Figure 86. Eastern Anatolian rug showing the irregularity of shape so common to the type. This feature has often been explained as characteristic of nomadic rugs in which the horizontal loom may be positioned in the ground and then taken up to be moved numerous times during the rug's time on the loom. Yet there are many Persian nomadic rugs that show no signs of irregularity.*

on an all wool foundation, there are several features that set them apart. They are far more likely to have dark wool wefts, and there is a characteristic edge finish in which the colours in the selvage alternate to give a simple design, often described as a chequer-board. The ends also often show fringe braided together in thick bands.

Many eastern Anatolian rugs are woven by nomads, and often these are characterised by an uneven shape or by wrinkling. This may be the result of the loom having been moved repeatedly during weaving.

Rugs from eastern Turkey made during the last half of the nineteenth century often use cochineal rather than madder for the reds. This gives a cooler red colour and one that results in a particular tonality with blue and green, frequently making the rugs darker than those of the Konya area. Rugs predating the mid-nineteenth century are more likely to show madder reds and a generally lighter colour tonality.

It is not always possible to localise these rugs well, and at times they are sold under the Yürük label, from a word referring to nomads. There is some controversy as to which of these rugs were woven by Kurdish people and which by Turkic nomads, and it is likely that a number of earlier rugs from this part of Anatolia were woven by Armenians before they were expelled at the beginning of the twentieth century (**Figures 84–88**).

Malatya, Diyarbekir, and Mardin are all collecting

*Figure 87. This four panel eastern Anatolian Kurd shows the dark colour scheme of this area. Most rugs of this type have ivory warps and dark wefts, with a colour scheme based around a cochineal red. The edges and ends show an elaborate finish.*

*Figure 88 (opposite). Three-medallion eastern Anatolian Kurd with characteristic fleecy wool. Several rugs of this type are known with Armenian inscriptions, suggesting possibly that it was a type woven by Armenians when they still constituted a large population in eastern Turkey.*

points for rugs, and it is extremely difficult to identify the sources of these rugs. Many are undoubtedly Kurdish products, as many parts of eastern Anatolia are predominantly Kurdish. The nomadism that has been common in this area for centuries is declining, although rug designs from this area have probably changed less than from any other part of Anatolia.

### Kars, Agri and Erzerum
These towns in the far north-eastern corner of

Turkey produce rugs that resemble those of the Caucasus in design and colours. They are all wool, with warps ranging from ivory to light brown, and the wool is the of the same variety as that on the rugs of Armenia. In considering rugs of this region, one must keep in mind that the borders between Turkey, Armenia, and Georgia were drawn for political reasons rather than as ethnically determined borders, which can account for the similarity of rugs from the region.

# CHAPTER 5

# Caucasian Rugs

Although rugs have long been woven by the indigenous peoples around the Caucasus mountains – a land roughly between the Black and Caspian Seas – those surviving examples of interest to the collector date from a period perhaps as early as the late sixteenth century into the early twentieth. During these years, Caucasian rugs have tended to share common features, including bold geometric designs and strong primary colours, in which red, blue, and ivory are prominent, with a relatively minor use of green, orange (usually a shade approaching apricot) and some mauve in earlier pieces. They are consistently symmetrically knotted, of low to medium knot density, and the use of cotton in the foundation is limited to a relatively small number of the more finely woven types.

Rugs have been woven in all three of the independent Caucasian republics: Azerbaijan, Armenia, and Georgia, with production also in the southern Russian Republic of Daghestan. The knotted pile carpet seems not to have become a major industry in this region until the last quarter of the nineteenth century, and it apparently lost any direct relationship to the folk art of the area after the Russian Revolution.

Production after the Second World War has been a strictly commercial undertaking.

## AZERBAIJAN

The rugs of Azerbaijan can probably best be described by district, and the most important include the areas around Kuba, Baku, Ganja, a broader district roughly centred on Shemakha, and the Nagorno Karabagh. A series of long rugs, usually described as runners in the West, was also produced in southern Azerbaijan. These rugs are difficult to identify by specific place or ethnic group. Some are described as coming from the Moghan Steppe, while others are identified with the Talysh, an Indo-Iranian speaking group living around Lenkoran. Some of these pieces are simply described as South Shirvan or Shirvan area, or perhaps by the Saliani label, after a town in the vicinity (**Figure 89**).

Rugs from the Kuba district in northern Azerbaijan are for the most part the most finely woven, and include types known in the West by the labels Perpedil, Chi-chi, Zejwa, Karagashli, and Konaghend (**Figures 90, 91 and 92**). The Perpedil

*Detail of Figure 89.*

*Figure 89. South Shirvan runner with repeating medallion figures and a heavily abrashed border. The designs are boldly geometric and the colours are strong. The specific origin of such rugs is difficult, as they were probably woven by various tribal groups over a wide area including the north-eastern parts of Persian Azerbaijan. The ethnic make-up of this region includes the Talysh, an Indo-European group that has probably occupied the same area for more than several thousand years, and the Azeri Turks, who arrived within the last thousand years.*

*Figure 90. Kuba district rug usually described as from the town of Perpedil. These are among the most finely woven of Caucasian rugs. The design, however, seems to be a simplified and heavily stylised rendition of one found on a group of seventeenth century rugs, probably from the Karabagh region.*

*Figure 91. Kuba district rug usually attributed to the town of Zejwa. Like the Perpedil design this also appears to be a rendition of motifs that appeared on an earlier group of Caucasian rugs, probably from the Karabagh region.*

*Figure 92 (opposite). Kuba district design often described as from the town of Konaghend. This design seems to be a geometric rendition of a Persian medallion design, and it obviously relates to some of the designs found on nineteenth century soumak rugs, particularly those from the town of Kusary, which is also part of the Kuba district.*

*Figure 94. Flatwoven bag from the Baku area showing designs often found on pile weaves. Such bags are known by a variety of terms in the Near East and are associated with the nomadic lifestyle. Often they are called bedding bags, but they were no doubt used to store and move a variety of household items.*

is perhaps best known and may achieve knot counts around 150 per square inch. The Chi-chi is characterised by a distinctive border. The town of Kusary has produced large, brightly coloured soumaks with powerful geometric designs (**Figure 93**). One may find cotton wefts on some Kuba rugs and even cotton used along the edges. Ends are often finished with the loose warp ends woven together into a thick protective band.

At one point carpet scholars theorised that Kuba was the source of a group of large Caucasian rugs, mostly from the seventeenth century and often described as the dragon rug group. This theory has now fallen into disfavour, as there is no real evidence that rugs were woven in the Kuba district prior to the nineteenth century. Indeed, among those surviving rugs from the Kuba district, there seems to be little

evidence that any of the designs went through a substantial period of evolution.

Baku is the largest city in Azerbaijan, and in its general vicinity there has been rug making probably since at least the eighteenth century. One well known type involves either the afshan or harshang design, usually on a blue field and with kufesque borders, which may reach over 12 feet (3.65 metres) in length. Some of these rugs show two shades of blue, unusual for the Caucasus. Rugs from this area may have cotton wefts. The Baku suburb of Saliani has woven rugs of repeating geometric figures. Many rugs of the region were formerly described as cabistans in the trade, although the term is seldom encountered now. There are also a number of pileless bags and trappings from this area (**Figure 94**).

In the Shirvan region, and villages to the west of

*Figure 93. Large red field soumak probably from the town of Kusary in the Kuba district. This area produced a large number of the popular red field nineteenth century soumaks, including those with designs of two and three medallions and even the so-called dragon soumaks.*

*Figure 96. White field prayer rug from the Shirvan area. This is probably the most frequently seen Caucasian prayer rug design and, like the Marasali, was no doubt produced over a period of more than a century. There are several dated examples from the turn of the nineteenth century, and some of the finest have silk warps.*

Baku and around the towns of Shemakha and Maraza, there are many different designs and local variants. Best known among them are the prayer rugs usually labelled as Marasali, with botehs on a blue field (**Figure 95**), and the white field prayer rug with stylised floral figures with lozenge-shaped compartments (**Figure 96**). These rugs often show excellent colours with lustrous wool, and

*Figure 95. Blue field prayer rug with a boteh design from the Shirvan area. Often these rugs are given the name Marasali and may be associated with the town of Maraza. Their production certainly covered a span of at least a century, and the earliest and finest may occasionally show silk warps.*

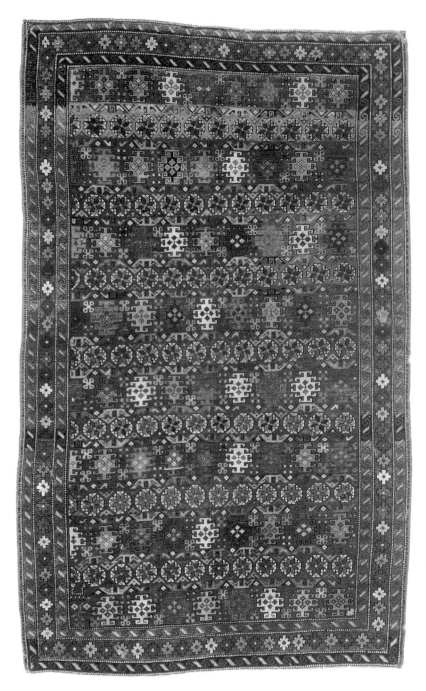

*Figure 97. Unusual Shirvan rug with small repeating figures. One often has the impression that the range of Shirvan designs is enormous, but after seeing some hundreds of these rugs it appears as though the same motifs are repeated over and over.*

*Figure 98 (opposite). Shirvan rug, late nineteenth century, with a design oriented in one direction. Rugs with these design elements appear to date from the end of the nineteenth century and cannot convincingly be assigned to a particular part of the Shirvan district.*

consequently have been sought by collectors. Some of them may date to the late eighteenth century, and occasionally one encounters a fine example with silk warps. Many other designs may be related to these two on the basis of structural characteristics and palette (**Figures 97 and 98**).

*Figure 99. Ganja rug with small figures arranged diagonally across the field. Rugs with this design are often labelled as from the Ganja area, but they are not clearly distinguishable from types of Kazak or Karabagh rugs.*
*Approx. 94 x 45ins. (239 x 114cm).*

*Figure 100 (opposite). Caucasian rug from the vicinity of Ganja with three medallions. This is a common design for rugs given the Ganja label. Such rugs are loosely woven on an all-wool foundation.*
*Approx. 93 x 55ins. (236 x 140cm).*

The area around Ganja has long been known for a thick, coarsely woven type of rug that may be indistinguishable from the Kazak, another grouping woven in western Azerbaijan and farther west in Armenia and southern Georgia (see under Armenia below for a description of the Kazak). Structurally the rugs usually described as the Ganja type may be more likely than the Kazak to have cotton either for the warp or weft, and the type has traditionally been described as favouring designs of diagonal stripes or diagonally arranged geometric figures. The type is poorly defined and could be seen simply as another variety of Kazak, They often have a lustrous wool and range from about 30 to 48 knots per square inch **(Figures 99 and 100).**

*Figure 101 (left). The design of this Karabagh rug is often attributed to the town of Lenkoran, although comparison with a number of rugs with this design shows that it seems to have had multiple sources within the Karabagh region.*

*Figure 102 (opposite). Karabagh rug with a narrow border and highly stylised floral figures. This type is difficult to localise, although it is probably from the area around Shusha.*

*Detail of Figure 102.*

Shusha is the major city of the Nagorno Karabagh district, and the region has a rich heritage of hand woven rugs that may date to the seventeenth century or earlier. Such well-known types as the sunburst and dragon Kazaks (the latter term is a misnomer, as they have nothing to do with Kazak rugs) were woven in this area, including other examples with large stylised palmettes often labelled as Lenkoran **(Figure 101)**. Rugs from the immediate vicinity of Shusha may show an unusual colour scheme, with an insect red, often combined with a relatively bright green. Large rugs were woven in the early nineteenth century around Shusha, often with such Persian patterns as the mina khani and herati **(Figure 102)**. A number of

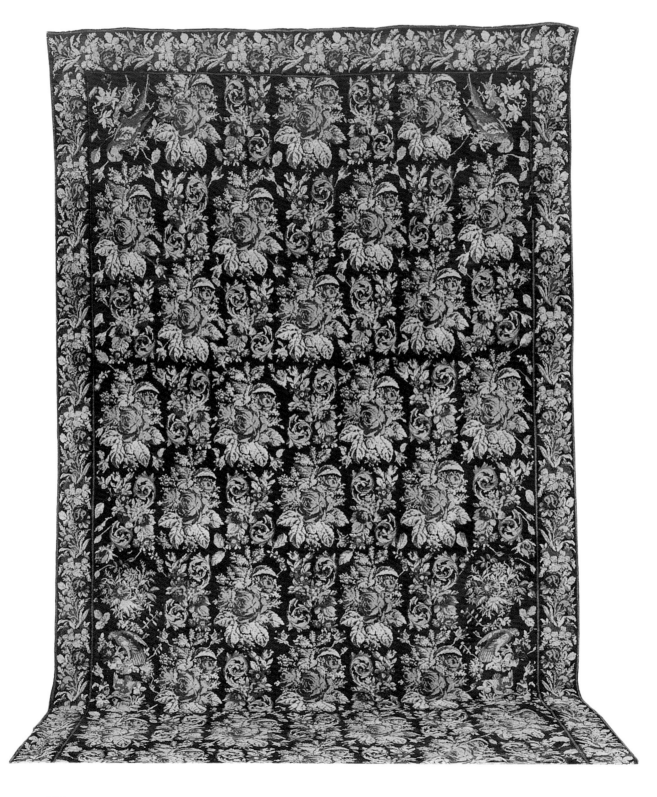

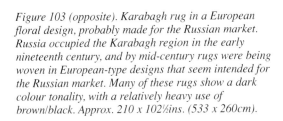

*Figure 103 (opposite). Karabagh rug in a European floral design, probably made for the Russian market. Russia occupied the Karabagh region in the early nineteenth century, and by mid-century rugs were being woven in European-type designs that seem intended for the Russian market. Many of these rugs show a dark colour tonality, with a relatively heavy use of brown/black. Approx. 210 x 102½ins. (533 x 260cm).*

*Figure 104. Karabagh long rug from the Shusha area. Many rugs in a runner format were woven in the Karabagh area, a large number of them showing Persian features. Approx. 109½ x 42ins. (278 x 107cm).*

pictorial rugs were also woven here during the late nineteenth century, and other rugs from the same period show designs for the Russian market (**Figure 103**). A number of long rugs from the Shusha district also show Armenian inscriptions (**Figures 104, 105 and 106**).

*Figure 105 (opposite left). Shusha long rug with repeating geometric figures. The city of Shusha produced a distinctive long rug during the last part of the nineteenth century. The design lexicon was eclectic, with many motifs borrowed from elsewhere.*

*Figure 106 (opposite right). Karabagh red field runner. Often this type shows reds from insect dyes, and many have Armenian inscriptions. Rugs with this design were obviously woven over a wide area, as they show a broad range of structural characteristics and subsidiary motifs.*

*Detail of Figure 106.*

The earliest surviving Azeri rugs that have been identified to date are a group that seem to have been woven in a single centre which produced rugs in Persian designs such as the avshan and harshang, as well as a series with a lattice and stylised animals, including dragons, in the interstices. These rugs are of controversial origin, but were probably produced in workshops established by Shah Abbas in the Karabagh region. They may reach about 20 feet (6.1 metres) in length, and often have pale red wefts. The wefts also show a peculiarity visible on the surface of a worn rug, where at intervals of a few inches up to perhaps seven inches an extra-thick cabled weft can be seen to cross the rug.

There are controversies around the rugs from this region, often focusing on the ethnic identity of the weavers. While it is often assumed that Azeris have been the major weavers, Armenians have been the major population group. Many of the rugs have Armenian inscriptions, particularly a number with sunburst designs and another design known as the cloudband. A number of the nineteenth century rugs have designs, including the sunburst and the so-called Lenkoran, that show a clear relationship to the dragon rugs of the seventeenth and eighteenth centuries.

With the dissolution of the Soviet Union, an armed rebellion occurred in the region, resulting in its currently becoming a *de facto* part of Armenia.

## ARMENIA

Armenian rugs have traditionally been described in the trade as Kazaks, and certainly Armenia has been one of the sources of this thick, coarsely knotted and boldly designed type of rug. They are all wool, symmetrically knotted, and characterised by bold, primary colours. The problem with specific labelling is that most Kazak rugs have been woven in an area between Erivan in Armenia and Tbilisi in Georgia,

107

*Figure 107 (opposite). Kazak rug with three medallions. This type is often attributed to the town of Lori-Pombak, although all the design elements, including the medallions and borders, may appear on Kazak rugs from other areas.*

*Figure 108. Kazak rug with a niche at one end. This type is often attributed to the town of Fachralo. These rugs often show a particularly prominent use of green. Although dates on Caucasian rugs are not common, unless they are Christian dates and part of an Armenian inscription, a relatively large number of this type are dated.*

while the western part of Azerbaijan protrudes into the same area. Towns and villages associated with these rugs may be of mixed population, as, for example, the Borchalo District, which is part of Georgia, but is inhabited mostly by Azeris. Other places associated with Kazak rugs include the towns of Kazak, Idjewan, Karachoph, Schulaver, and Fachralo, which also have mixed populations. It is probably best to label these rugs without specific reference to an ethnic group. **(Figures 107, 108 and 109)**.

*Figure 109. Rugs of this design are often described as shield Kazaks, and they show great variability. Like most other common Caucasian designs they are likely to have been woven in a number of villages.*

*Figure 110. Kazak prayer rug, probably from the vicinity of Borchalo. Surviving Kazak prayer rugs must date back at least a century and a half, if not much further, but the majority seem to have been woven around the turn of the nineteenth century. Earlier pieces are more likely to be larger than later pieces, with geometric motifs on a red field.*

Rugs from the Borchalo district are probably the most distinctive of the area, and they often show the boldest designs. While the field is often divided into three or more medallions, the borders frequently show a design in which diagonal lines zigzag from one side to the next. The colour schemes often contain more ivory than is found in other parts of the Caucasus, with a major use of red, usually less blue, and smaller yellow patches (**Figure 110**). The wool is particularly fleecy, and the wefts are a pale red or yellow in the earlier pieces, and some of the later pieces have blue wefts. Large rugs with a 2-1-2 design, with a large central medallion and two smaller ones at each end, are often given the Karachoph label, although a number of pieces in this design are woven in the Borchalo area. There are also a number of prayer rugs from this area.

Two Kazak designs have in recent decades attracted great collector enthusiasm. The so-called star Kazak and the pinwheel Kazak are popular items at auction, and some examples are dated to the eighteenth century, although evidence for this is scanty.

## GEORGIA

Until recently Georgian rugs have received little attention, but it is now recognised that there is a long tradition of weaving in many parts of the country. Fragments of pile carpets and flatweaves dating to the fourteenth century, perhaps even earlier, have been excavated from Georgian caves, occupied during various of the Mongol incursions. As caves may be drier than areas exposed to rain, the survival rate of objects of wood and wool is increased.

The Borchalo District in the south produces the coarsely knotted, boldly coloured Kazak type of rug. The weavers here are primarily Azeris, but there are many Georgians as well, and similar rugs are produced by Georgians in the central part of the country.

In the outlying mountainous regions there is also a long tradition of kilim weaving, including a type from the Tushetia region in which black and green are unusually prominent (**Figure 111**). The kilims often involve large stylised floral figures. Rarely one will find an inscribed kilim in the Georgian script.

*Figure 111 (opposite). Caucasian kilim from the Tushetia region of Georgia. The colour scheme of these pieces differs markedly from those woven in Azerbaijan or Armenia, although they are structurally the same. At least one kilim is known with an elaborate Georgian inscription.*

*Detail of Figure 111.*

*Figure 112 (opposite). This rug from the Derbent area shows the typical dark blue edges and ends. The design is based upon highly stylised flowers.*

*Figure 113. Derbent rug with a border associated with Chi-chi rugs and opposed vases with highly stylised floral figures. These are generally of a coarser weave than rugs made slightly to the south in the Kuba district. Rather than show the tight cotton side selvage often found on Kuba rugs, these pieces are more likely to have a looser selvage of dark blue wool.*

## DAGHESTAN

Unlike Azerbaijan, Armenia, and Georgia, the administrative region of Daghestan is not independent and is still part of Russia, although there has been a separatist movement. In numerous towns and villages around the city of Derbent there was a major rug weaving industry, particularly during the last quarter of the nineteenth century and the first quarter of the twentieth. These pieces are not as finely woven as those of the Kuba District, but share many of the same designs. The colours tend to be slightly darker than those of other Caucasian rugs. Many show edge selvages of dark blue wool, while most are in small scatter sizes with some runners (**Figures 112, 113 and 114**). Rugs

*Figure 114. Derbent rug with a design showing crab-like figures often described as an alpan design. This design may also appear on rugs from the Kuba district, but those from the Derbent area are more likely to show a prominent use of blue.*

*Figure 115 (opposite). Rugs from Zeykhur and nearby villages in the Derbent region often show designs influenced by Europe and were probably woven for the Russian market. Many show a wide range of relatively intense colours, and the designs include realistically drawn flowers and medallions with radiating arms suggestive of the Karabagh sunburst.*

from the Tabasaran area of southern Daghestan, around the town of Zeykhur, are rather loosely woven, but show an unusual range of designs ranging from stylised flowers to a dramatic sunburst-like design. Some also show adaptations of European design, probably a result of Russian influence (**Figure 115**).

A group of rugs assigned to the Avars and Kumyks is from Daghestan. These are largely blue field compositions with geometric figures in red, often at least twice as long as they are wide. Flatweaves of the same designs are known, and many show small traces of synthetic colour, suggesting that the group does not have early antecedents.

For many years a type of ivory field Shirvan prayer rug was erroneously labelled as a Daghestan, although it has now been recognised as originating from the same region as the Marasali prayer rugs.

A number of embroideries are known from Daghestan.

## MODERN CAUCASIAN RUGS

The Caucasian rug industry was revived after the Second World War, but it never recaptured its former popularity. Indeed, the Caucasian carpet had changed dramatically in both its appearance and the manner in which it was produced.

While the earlier Caucasian rug was basically the product of cottage industries, the later industry was based around large manufactories in which hundreds of weavers worked. The foundations of the new rugs were all cotton rather than the wool formerly used. The dyes became a good grade of synthetic, but this was accomplished in such a manner as to leave no colour variation, and the interesting abrash of earlier rugs was eliminated. In fact, the colours were rather dull, while the designs also became so standardised that the manager of a factory could order production based upon a number from the design book. This took away the spontaneity of the earlier rugs, in which the small subsidiary figures supplementing the main design were often arranged so that they differed in size and placement from one side of the field to the next. The weavers were no longer required to demonstrate any creativity, but could simply follow the scale paper drawings in which the design was laid out with perfect side-to-side symmetry.

What this meant was that the human influence in these rugs was filtered out. What began as a peasant folk art, became the product of an industry, but an industry in which the weavers were not replaced by machines, probably because machines would have been more expensive. These rugs have not been very successful on the market, and other places borrowing Caucasian designs have produced more appealing rugs. There are now rugs in Caucasian designs from Pakistan that resemble more closely the original models than recent production from the Caucasus.

# CHAPTER 6

# TURKMEN RUGS AND RUGS FROM AFGHANISTAN

The Turkmen are a Turkic speaking group which possibly began their westward migration with the Huns of the third and fourth centuries, although they arrived at their present locations at a later date. They eventually settled in the area that now comprises modern Turkmenistan, with some also living in adjoining parts of north-eastern Iran and north-western Afghanistan. This area generally covers the territory east of the Caspian Sea, extending to the Amu Darya river, while some Turkmen also live in western Uzbekistan.

Turkmen rugs have fascinated collectors, as the earliest surviving types can usually be identified as to tribe from peculiarities of design and structure. Their characteristic tribal motifs are usually octagonal, mostly quartered, and often specific to a particular group. These motifs are called guls, probably derived from a Persian word for flower, and slight variations in their detailing are significant in identifying the tribe that wove a particular rug. Pile weaves of the Turkmen also reflect the nomadic lifestyle, and even late nineteenth century commercial rugs can have the same format as rugs that were made for use in and around the tent.

Citizens of modern Turkmenistan take pride in their tribal origins, and it is not only rugs, but also many aspects of costume, which are specific to certain tribal groups. There are Turkmen guls on the flag of Turkmenistan, and rug motifs are often found on public buildings in the capital, Ashghabat.

## THE TEKKE

The Tekke Turkmen are the most numerous and important of the Turkmen groups, and a large percentage of Turkmen rugs to reach the West have been woven by the Tekke. They have lived around the oases of Merv and Tedjend, as well as in the strip of well-watered land at the base of the Kopet Dagh mountains which form the border with Iran. Their rugs are extremely finely woven with the asymmetrical knot, open to the right, on an all-wool foundation, although at times there are small patches of silk pile in the finest pieces. The main carpet of the Turkmen yurt, or circular felt tent, by tradition measured in the range of 5½–9 feet (1.67–2.74 metres), and Tekke main carpets are characterised by the repetition of a specific gul, repeated in rows across the field. Between the larger guls there is a series of minor guls that nearly fill the intergul spaces, and the field, which is essentially always red, varies from a deep brick red to a paler rust (**Figure 116**). The main gul is probably the best known of all Turkmen ornaments, and has frequently been copied in other weaving areas.

The Tekkes weave a number of other types as well as main carpets. A format allegedly made to be used

*Figure 116. Tekke main carpet with four vertical rows of typical major guls and extra panels at each end. The main border shows substantial variation, and this feature is usually simplified on later rugs. While there are only slight variations in the shape of the main gul, there can be several distinct types of secondary gul.*

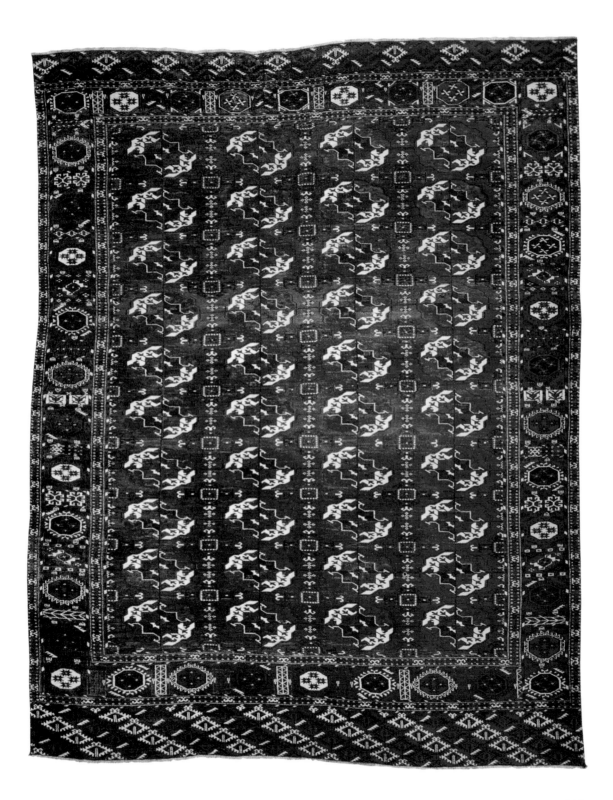

119

*Figure 117. Tekke ensi with a single niche at the top. While the major border may be of several types and the quadrants may even be bisected by additional vertical stripes, in some examples there are other features, such as the appearance and position of the arch, that are relatively constant. These differ substantially in the density of the knotting.*

as the door flap of the yurt is known as the ensi, and this has a quartered field with a niche at the top and extra bands of design across the bottom. The niche suggests that at times these may have been used as prayer rugs **(Figure 117)**. Other Turkmen tribes also weave ensis, but they all show slightly different designs within the same basic format.

Tekke tent bags are popular with collectors. In most cases the plain weave backs have already been removed, and only the pile-woven bag face is retained. These usually involve the repetition of smaller guls than one finds on main carpets, and they are more varied in details **(Figures 118, 119 and 120)**. The finest knotting on Tekke rugs is reserved for several

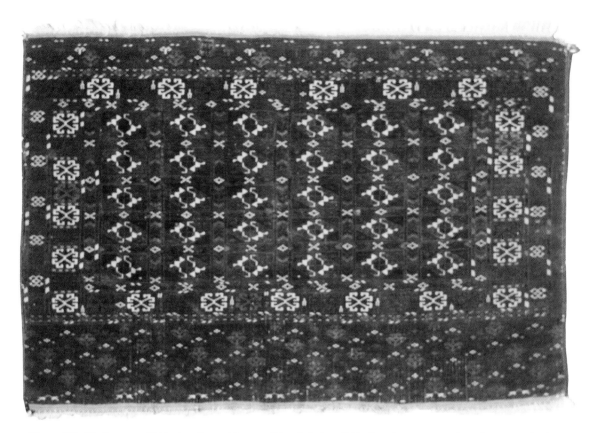

*Figure 118. Finely woven Tekke bag face with a traditional design. Tekke bag faces are consistently among the finest Turkmen weaves, at times reaching a knot count in the vicinity of 400 knots per square inch. Although many consider Salor rugs to be the most artistic Turkmen rugs, they are seldom as finely woven.*

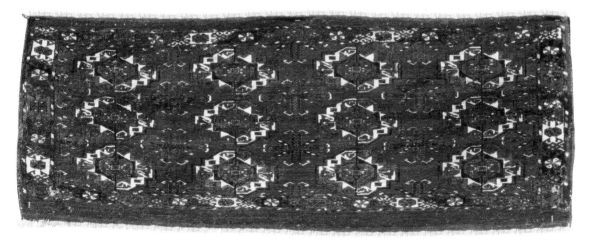

*Figure 119. Tekke torba with twelve typical bag face guls. These are also often among the most finely woven Tekkes, and although they may appear to vary only within a small range, collectors of these pieces are able to identify many small differences in design that are the subject of debate among specialists.*

*Figure 120 (opposite above). Tekke bag face with a gul that may also appear on Salor and Saryk bags. This is the kind of Tekke bag most likely to show patches of magenta silk. In the earlier rug literature the gul was consistently associated with Salor weaving, and at other times with the Merv Oasis, where Tekkes, Saryks, and Salors have lived at various times. Clearly, however, it was also woven by the western Tekkes in the Ashghabat area.*

*Figure 121 (opposite below). Saryk bag with major guls that may appear on Salor or Tekke work. The Saryk identification is made from structural features, including the symmetrical knots. Some of these pieces have patches of both white cotton and magenta silk. Approx. 58 x 37½ins. (148 x 95 cm).*

*Figure 122 (right). Saryk ensi with an unusual amount of silk highlighting. Note the row of niches along the top. Earlier examples are a deep rich red, often with small amounts of cotton used for the areas of white pile. Late examples may be dark, with a field that may even be dark brown, and these are more likely to be asymmetrically knotted.*

types of bag, some of which show patches of silk.

Rugs of the Tekkes probably had not reached western markets in significant numbers before the Russian conquest of Central Asia. Not long after the battle of Geok Tepe in 1881, in which the Tekke armies were overwhelmingly defeated by a Russian force, Turkmen rugs and those of the Tekke in particular began to reach the West. They quickly achieved a certain popularity, and the Tsarist government took enough interest in Central Asian crafts, and carpets in particular, that several expeditions were sent to bring back the finest examples. Our understanding of these rugs is based in large part upon several important early Russian publications.

## THE SARYK

While the Saryk appear to be related to the Tekke, rugs of the two tribes differ structurally. The symmetrical knot is essentially never found on a Tekke rug, but most of the earliest Saryks are symmetrically knotted, although they are seldom as fine as Tekke rugs. By the late nineteenth century the asymmetrical knot appears to have been used as frequently as the symmetrical, but by this time the rugs were often very dark in colour, and some have questioned whether they were actually woven by the Saryk. White highlights of cotton often appear on Saryk rugs, probably most frequently on late pieces, and some have patches of pale magenta silk. Both early and late Saryks tend to have slightly depressed alternate warps giving them a ribbed appearance on the back.

There are at least three different guls used on Saryk main carpets, and several guls are used on bags (**Figure 121**). Unlike the Tekke ensi, the Saryk ensi shows a row of niches across the top (**Figure 122**). The Saryk as well as the Salor appear to be related to

*Figure 123. Salor main carpets are often larger than those of other tribes. These show little abrash or variation in the design. It is difficult to think of these as nomadic rugs, and it seems likely that they were woven in a workshop, perhaps at some point in the Merv oasis at a time when it was controlled by the Salor. Approx. 128½ x 102ins. (326 x 259cm).*

*Figure 124. Salor bag with a similar gul to those appearing on Tekke and Saryk bags, although the structure here, with the asymmetrical knot open to the left and the double-warped structure allows, identification as to tribal source.*

the Tekkes, and they are thought in earlier centuries to have been much more numerous and important than they were by the late nineteenth century. The Tekke expansion came mostly in the nineteenth century, but because of the subsequent Russian expansion into Central Asia, their dominance did not last long.

## THE SALOR

While Salor rugs are usually not so finely woven as the early Tekke pieces, they are thought by many to include the most artistically successful Turkmen rugs, with strong colours – usually with little abrash – and a graceful spacing of motifs, that has prompted many collectors to assign some of them to a particularly early date. A particular quartered gul with two animal figures in each quadrant is characteristic of Salor main

carpets, which are often larger than those of the Tekke and Saryk (**Figure 123**). The bags may show similar guls to those of the Saryk, and it is theorised that the tribes are closely related (**Figure 124**). Structurally, however, they are woven with the asymmetrical knot and differ from Tekke examples in that the knots are usually open to the left. Even more than the Saryk examples, these rugs are double-warped and thus less flexible than the Tekke rug.

Ensis of the Salor, which are thought to number less than a dozen survivors, have become particularly sought by collectors. After they were driven from the Merv oasis by the Tekkes in the mid-nineteenth century, the Salor became scattered, with some settling farther south along the Murghab River, while others settled in Sarakhs on the Persian border.

*Figure 126. Chaudor ensis of several different types are known. Note the halved ertmen guls in the lower cross panel. There are also Chaudor prayer rugs in a non-ensi format.*

*Figure 127. This is a rare type of bag for valuables, and at times it is used as a Koran cover. When open it is square, and it is closed by folding each corner inward, producing a smaller square shape. This example is Yomut work.*

## THE CHAUDOR AND ARABATCHI

The Chaudor live in a number of locations within Turkmenistan. The tribe was known as the one more likely than any other to take in outsiders as members. The Chaudor are now mostly to be found along the upper Amu Darya River, somewhat north of the Arabatchi, to whom they are probably related. Many Chaudor main carpets show a characteristic non-quartered gul called the ertmen, and rugs with this design usually do not have a minor gul (**Figure 125**). Chaudors also may show a quartered gul with a small animal or two in each quadrant, and these are usually described as tauk noshka guls. These rugs are characterised by a purplish brown field and a pale red approaching a salmon colour (**Figure**s **126 and 127**). Most show at least some cotton wefts.

*Figure 125 (opposite). Chaudor main carpet with the classic ertmen gul. Typically these rugs show diagonal rows of guls with slightly varying colours; there are no minor guls. Most Chaudors have dark wool warps, and many of the rugs show a substantial use of cotton in the weft. Rarely one finds an example with the field in the salmon red and the guls in the purplish brown.*

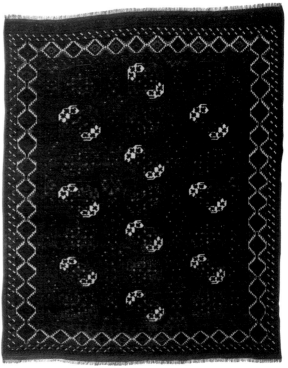

*Figure 128. Arabatchi chuvals (large tent bags) are rare and often show an enlarged Tekke-like gul with a dark tonality. In the western rug literature the Arabatchi label appeared only several decades ago, as the tribe is relatively small, and the rugs had never become well known. Approx. 26½ x 55ins. (67 x 140cm).*

*Figure 129. Ersari rug from Afghanistan of a type usually marketed as 'Afghan' in the West. These are coarsely woven with a thick pile. There are nearly a dozen different types of gul, some of which almost certainly have a tribal significance, although no coherent labels have yet emerged.*

The Arabatchi also often use the tauk noshka gul, but their range of colours is generally somewhat more sombre. They wove an ensi with a stripe of animal figures along the bottom. Their bags, which are relatively rare, may be identified from their colour (**Figure 128**).

## THE ERSARI

This is a widely dispersed tribe ranging from southern Turkmenistan and Uzbekistan to northern Afghanistan. It was alleged to be the first Turkmen group to become sedentary, and the rugs – while often colourful and charming – are usually the least finely woven of all Turkmen types. The typical main carpet has large octagonal guls, usually quartered, with thick pile and often a goat hair selvage along the edges. There are many subtribes, but it is unclear whether they can be identified by specific tribal guls (**Figures 129 and 130**).

*Figure 130. Ersari rug with large guls arranged diagonally. There are many types with different features within the same basic format. Modern rugs of this type may be somewhat larger, to fit room sizes in the West, and often the colours have become less varied so that one finds only red and black or dark blue. Approx. 138 x 94½ins. (350 x 240cm).*

*Figure 131. Ersari flatwoven bag from Afghanistan. While the basic structure is of wool, the design is rendered in silk.*

Like other Turkmen tribes, the Ersari weave ensis, with or without niches at the top, and they have produced a wide variety of bags which are usually larger than those of the other tribes. Many of the bags are flatwoven, at times with parts of the design rendered in silk thread in yellow, pale red, blue, and green (**Figure 131**).

An area east of the middle Amu Darya in Uzbekistan has been known as the source of rugs that have been marketed under the Beshir label, after the name of one of the villages where they were woven. The weavers are not all Ersaris, but an ethnic mix, and the designs of these rugs include eclectic borrowings from Persian and other sources. As the Beshir rug seldom includes designs that in any sense could be described as tribe related, one should probably see these as village rugs (**Figures 132, 133 and 134**). A number of Ersari-related

*Figure 132 (right). One quarter of a large Beshir rug with a design adapted from Persian repeating patterns. Some of these rugs exceed 18 feet (5.5 metres) in length, and were almost certainly intended for export. Considering, however, that there are some bag faces and tent trappings of the Beshir type, there is some question as to how much the Beshir was commercial and how much a tribal rug.*

*Figure 133 (below). Beshir bag based on an ikat design. This appears to be a Beshir weave in a format suggesting use as a bag face, although the design itself is based upon Uzbeki ikats and would seem to have no particular significance to the Turkmen.*

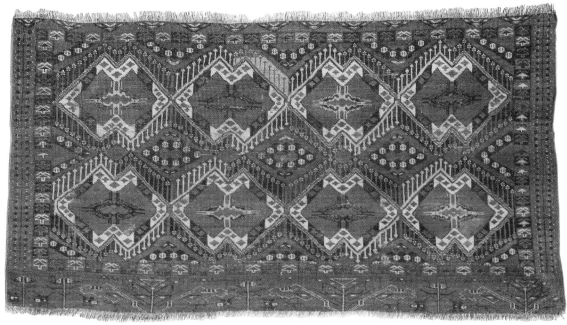

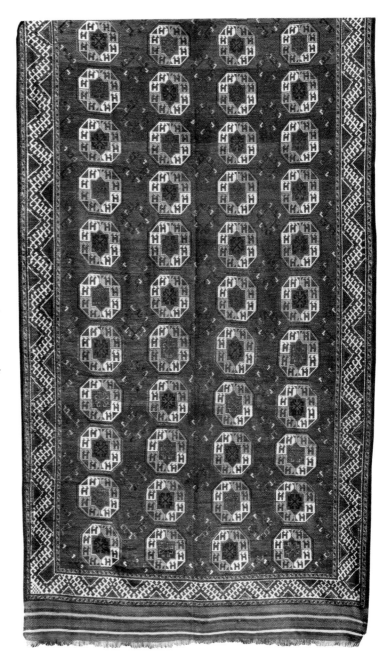

*Figure 134 (opposite). Beshir prayer rugs are often narrow and show an ivory field with small repeating figures. The niche at the top is usually small. Approx. 91 x 52½ins. (231 x 133cm).*

*Figure 135. Large Kizil Ayak rug with two animal figures in each quadrant of the guls. The Kizil Ayak are a poorly studied group that some scholars believed are related to the Tekkes and others see as an Ersari-related tribe. Their rugs have a distinctive appearance, and most seem to be woven in variants of this gul.*

tribes, such as the Kizil Ayak, also weave rugs in a slightly different range of designs **(Figure 135)**. Some designs from this area are based on the silk ikat designs more closely associated with Uzbeki crafts.

## THE YOMUT

The Yomut are a large group scattered from north-eastern Iran, where the largest groups live, to the part of Turkmenistan east of the Caspian and several areas around the Amu Darya. Some Yomut have been

133

*Figure 136. Yomut main carpet with the common kepse gul. These rugs usually have a browner tonality than the Tekke, Salor, and Ersari types. They are symmetrically knotted. While Tekkes are most likely to show a pileless kilim band at both ends, with no trace of design, the bands at each end of Yomut carpets are most likely to be of pile with a range of different repeating designs.*

*Figure 137 (opposite). Unusual Yomut ensi in that it does not show a quartered field. This example shows a Tekke-like arch at the top, although some Yomut ensis have no arch. It is interesting to note that all Turkmen tribes seem to have a characteristic ensi design, all of which show features unique to the particular tribe. Oddly enough tribes alleged to be closely related often have dramatically differing ensis. Ensis of the Salor, Saryk and Tekke, for example, differ significantly. Approx. 61 x 50ins. (155 x 127cm).*

sedentary longer than groups such as the Tekke, and they have been both farmers and participants in the trans-Caspian trade.

Yomut rugs are more likely to have a brownish rather than a red field, and the larger pieces in particular are more likely to be symmetrically knotted. There are a number of relatively large guls, some of which appear to be adaptations of palmettes from Persian rugs. Often there are no minor guls, and the border is more likely to have an ivory field than other Turkmen rugs. Rather than the long plain weave ends seen in Tekke, Saryk, and Salor rugs, one is more likely to find an extra band of pile weave at each end **(Figures 136 and 137)**.

*Figure 138. Small Yomut bag face with unusual ovoid guls; the brown field is typical of the type. Ovoid guls are uncommon and appear mostly on bags. It is not clear whether they have any particular tribal significance.*

*Figure 139. Yomut ok-bash. When assembled it forms a bag for tent pegs or, according to some sources, spindles. These pieces probably have a long history among the Turkmen, and show a limited range of designs. It is not clear whether there are examples of the type from other Turkmen tribes.*

*Figure 140. Yomut asmalyk, a trapping used in the Turkmen wedding ceremony. These occur in a limited range of designs, but most surviving examples were woven by the Yomut. Approx. 31½ x 49ins. (80 x 125cm).*

*Detail of Figure 140.*

Yomut bags are perhaps more varied than those of the other tribal groups, with a number of different guls **(Figures 138 and 139)**. A five-sided trapping known as an asmalyk is most common from the Yomut, although smaller numbers are known from other tribes. These have been traditionally used in the Turkmen wedding ceremony **(Figure 140)**.

There are probably more Yomut tent bands than are

Figure 141. Turkmen pile tent bands often range over 39 feet (12 metres) in length and about 12ins. (30cm) wide. While the ivory part of this example is flatwoven, the design is in finely knotted pile. The pileless tent bands, usually woven in a warp float technique, are more variable in width and design. There are a number of different types woven by the Yomut and the Ersari, but it is unclear whether pileless tent bands were woven by the Salor, Saryk, and Tekke tribes.
Approx. 491 x 12ins. (1248 x 30cm).

Figure 142 (opposite). The Sunday market in Turkmenistan's capital, Ashghabat, where weavers from nearby Turkmen tribes sell both old and new rugs. Here one can see Yomuts from the west and Ersaris from as far away as Kerki selling different types of Turkmen rugs. Embroideries and wedding coats made for Turkmen women can be found for sale here.

found from other tribes **(Figure 141)**. The most elaborate of these are finely knotted over every other warp on a long narrow loom that leaves a completed band of up to 50 feet (15.24 metres). These are used to decorate the bridal tent during the first year of a marriage. Surviving tent bands of this type, while never numerous, are also known from other tribes as well, particularly the Tekke. Other types of bands without pile are woven in several types of warp substitution weave and are often used like barrel hoops to give the tent structural integrity.

## RUGS FROM AFGHANISTAN

Unlike Turkmenistan, where most of the population is Turkmen, Afghanistan is multi-ethnic. The dominant population is described as Pashtun, probably a mixture of Turkic and indigenous Indo-Iranian peoples. There is a population of ethnic Iranians in the west, a large group of Mongoloid appearance within the central mountain mass of the country, nomadic

Baluchi in the western and southern deserts, and a mixture of Uzbekis and Turkmen in the north. Many Turkmen are relatively recent arrivals. They migrated into Afghanistan after the Russians established control over Turkmenistan, and more came after the Soviets seized power.

Most of these people seem to have been from the Ersari group, although the exact relationships among such peoples as the Kizil Ayak, the Chub Bash, and the Saltiq are unclear. They are pastoralists and, as in Turkmenistan, they are weavers. They have produced the same kinds of thick, coarsely-knotted rugs with large rectangular guls that one finds in the Karshi area north of the Amu Darya. A number of different guls are used, but they are seldom clearly associated with specific tribes.

During the last half of the twentieth century many Ersari rugs, called Afghans in the trade, evolved in slightly different directions in Afghanistan, where they were often larger than the traditional sizes.

*Figure 143. Uzbeki suzanis show elaborate floral designs embroidered on ivory ground. They are now usually sought by the same collectors interested in pile carpets, although the designs show little relationship to those of Central Asian carpets. Suzanis form an important part of the dowry of a young Uzbeki woman. Approx. 100 x 64½ins. (253 x 164cm).*

Because some are double-warped, they are thicker as well. Colours have deviated somewhat more from the typical red field, and some Afghan rugs may even have a yellow field. Among recent Afghan rugs one also finds a small number with designs associated with the Beshir, including types that are apparently unique to Afghanistan.

A small number of Tekkes and Saryks live north of Herat, and their rugs are more finely woven than other Afghan carpets. In addition to traditional designs, there has been a small production of finely knotted rugs in Persian patterns.

The nomadic Baluchi of western and southern Afghanistan weave a distinctive variety of rug, usually somewhat less finely knotted than the Baluchi rugs of Iran and showing less blue. There is a dark Baluchi type that may even exceed 12 feet (3.65 metres) in length, and there are many Baluchi prayer rugs. A tree-of-life field design is common, and there are many rugs in which simple geometric motifs are repeated across the field. White may be used dramatically as a highlight, particularly on some of the saddlebag faces. Like Baluchi rugs from Iran, they are asymmetrically knotted on a wool foundation, usually with a dark camel hair selvage on the edges. The kilim ends may show rows of brocade or plain weave stripes.

The Uzbekis of northern Afghanistan were probably less involved than the Turkmen in carpet weaving, but they weave many large kilims in slit tapestry or an unusual interlocking structure. They also produce embroidered suzanis, which have recently become popular with rug collectors (**Figure 143**), as well as colourful silk fabrics in ikat, a resist dyeing technique (**Figure 144**). Some Uzbekis have become involved in the Turkmen rug industry, producing thick red rugs of the traditional Afghan type.

*Figure 144. Uzbeki ikat, a silk fabric made in a resist dyeing technique. Ikat designs are often adapted for use on Ersari rugs. Earlier ikats are more likely to have cotton warps, while later pieces are all silk or, in the latest pieces, all rayon. There are also velvet fabrics made in the ikat technique.*

There are also small groups of Arab weavers in northern Afghanistan who weave a coarse, all wool double-warped rug, in which alternate warps are separated by wefts so that one shed of warps lies anterior to (or above) the other shed. As the knots are tied over only the upper shed of warps, the design is barely visible on the back of the rug. These pieces are woven in narrow strips that are sewn together to make a larger rug (**Figure 145**).

Unusual rugs are also woven by various Kirghiz groups within Afghanistan and Central Asia. There is a type of Kirghiz rug woven around the Uzbeki city of Andijan in which there is only a single weft between the rows of knots.

There are many smaller ethnic groups within Afghanistan that make flatweaves (**Figure 146**).

Afghan refugees from camps in Pakistan began weaving 'war rugs', soon after the Soviet invasion of 1979. Woven like typical Afghans, they show non-traditional pictorial designs with tanks, helicopters, and other instruments of war.

The disruptions in Afghanistan following the Soviet invasion and the many years of civil war following the Soviet withdrawal in 1989 have all brought about major changes in the rug industry. There has not been a time in the last several decades when there were no refugee camps, and consequently Afghan labour in such places has been plentiful and inexpensive. Large numbers of inexpensive rugs have thus reached western markets, usually labelled as Baluchis, although most were probably made by Pashtuns and other peoples. These rugs are dark, with shades of brown, deep reds, dark blue, and a small amount of white for highlights. Many are larger than the traditional Baluchi rug, and they often show unusual designs in which pictorial elements are prominent.

In several areas there have been successful attempts to re-establish natural dyeing, and this has produced some excellent rugs in traditional designs, often in a slightly finer weave than the originals.

In view of the most recent upheavals in Afghanistan, it is difficult to predict how the Afghan industry will evolve during the next decades.

---

*Figure 145. Arab rug from Afghanistan. This type is knotted only on the top shed of warps, and thus the design shows only faintly on the back. Often these have been labelled as Uzbeki work, but groups on both sides of the border between Uzbekistan and Afghanistan known to weave these rugs are of Arab descent.*

*Figure 146 (opposite). These double bags were made by a small group called the Lorghabi, whose exact ethnic origins are unknown. They may be Uzbeki related or of mixed origin. The same group also makes pile weaves in similar designs but with more sombre colours.*

# CHAPTER 7

# RUGS FROM CHINA AND THE FAR EAST

The traditional rugs of China are usually distinguishable from those of western Asia at a glance. Red is seldom used, and when it appears it is pale. Blue is much more common, and some Chinese rugs have three or four different shades of blue, usually set against a yellow or ivory ground. Subsidiary colours such as green and orange are unusual. The export of Chinese rugs to the West was slow to develop, but some appear to have reached Europe after 1860 when European armies looted the Summer Palace near Beijing. Forty years later another army from Europe and America looted the Imperial City, after foreign diplomats had been besieged during the Boxer Rebellion. While Chinese rugs were thus introduced into Europe and America, they did not begin to reach western markets in significant numbers until the First World War interrupted trade with the Near East, and European and American importers needed another source of merchandise.

Fragments of carpets extending back to the first half of the first millennium A.D. have been found in the deserts of Xinjiang, China's western-most province. Because many of these examples seem more to resemble the work of western Asia, and many of them have been found in sites associated with the silk route, there has been some question as to whether these rugs were woven by the Chinese or various of the Turkic or Iranian groups who dominated central Asia until relatively recent historical times. There are theories that China learned rug weaving from traders or migrants from the Near East, while other theories speculate that weaving was introduced into the Persian world by westward migrants from central Asia.

The carpet fragments, for the most part, show little relationship to Chinese rugs of the last several centuries. Ancestors of the modern Chinese rug probably predate the seventeenth century, although dating of early pieces is controversial, as there are no relevant pieces with an inwoven date and no support in early inventories. During the reign of the Emperor Kang Hsi (A.D.1661–1722), however, French Jesuits at his court accompanied him on a visit to the western provinces, and there at Ningxia and Tatung they noted the manufacture of carpets that they compared to those of Turkey. Partially based on this information, early surviving Chinese rugs are often described as from Ningxia.

Compared with Persian products of the same period, most Chinese rugs are coarsely woven, with the asymmetrical knot usually on a cotton foundation, although there are rare exceptions in which wool may appear in either the warp or weft. They occur in a wide range of sizes and are generally more flexible than rugs of Iran. The knotting seldom exceeds about 30 asymmetrical knots per square inch, although some silk rugs are finer. Yet unlike the typical Persian silk rug, the warp and weft even of these rugs is likely to be cotton rather than silk. Many thought to be the earliest have a characteristic brown colour around all four sides that has often eroded so that little pile is left, even though the rest of the rug may be intact. Designs may be floral, geometric, or include dragons or folions. Despite the relatively coarse knotting, the drawing of floral figures is often surprisingly graceful, with renditions of peonies, the lotus, and chrysanthemums. **(Figures 147, 148, 149 and 150.)**

*Figure 147. Many of the earliest surviving Chinese rugs, probably woven in Ningxia, show austere designs with stylised dragons and repeating geometric forms.*

*Figure 148 (opposite). Ningxia floral rug with peonies. The loose texture and fleecy wool place this among the Ningxia production, based around traditional motifs.*

*Figure 149. Ningxia rug with bats. Bats appear on some of the earliest surviving Chinese rugs, as they have a well understood symbolic meaning referring to luck or good fortune.*

*Figure 150. Ningxia Chinese rug with a small central medallion, probably from the late nineteenth century when Ningxia rugs were drifting away from the formal rigidity of the type with eroded brown borders.*
*Approx. 55 x 29ins. (140 x 74cm).*

*Figure 151 (opposite left). Column rug from the Ningxia region of China. When wrapped around a column, the coils of the dragon appear to be continuous. In the main reception hall of the Imperial Palace in Beijing similar dragons are drawn encircling the largest columns closest to the throne platform. The dragon was symbolic of the emperor. Approx. 126½ x 66½ins. (321 x 169cm).*

*Figure 152 (opposite right). Chinese saddle rug, woven in two pieces with the pile slanting downward on both sides. Early Chinese paintings show that this type of saddle rug has been used for well over a thousand years. Some Tang dynasty figures show a horse and rider in which there is a clearly delineated saddle rug.*

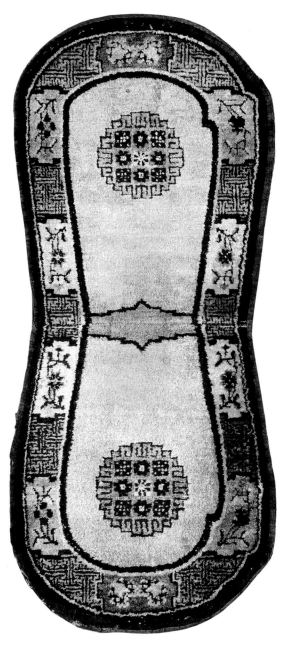

Several unique types are found among early Chinese rugs. Perhaps most interesting are the pillar rugs, woven for Buddhist temples where the large columns supporting the roof are covered with rugs on which the sides have no borders and are joined together (**Figure 151**). When a dragon design is used, it thus seems to coil around the column. Another Chinese type is a distinctive kind of saddle rug, woven in two pieces and sewn together at the middle so that the pile slants downward on both sides (**Figure 152**). Yet another type unique to China and Tibet

*Figure 153. Square compartments were woven in Ningxia as seats for Buddhist monks in monasteries.*

*Figure 154.
Ningxia rug with a
classic running
swastika border
and a repeating
field pattern.*

is made up of squares in a long runner-like rug. The squares are thought to represent places for the monks in Buddhist monasteries to meditate **(Figure 153)**.

By the early twentieth century the carpet industry was, to a large extent, controlled by westerners, who supplied designs suggestive of a Chinese source, but were more attuned to needs of distant markets. Colour schemes evolved, and the rugs became much thicker and stiffer in texture **(Figure 154)**. By this time, rug weaving mostly took place in larger cities in eastern China. The Beijing rug, often with a dark blue field, remained closer to Chinese tradition. Rugs woven in and around the port city of Tianjin were more likely to be double-warped and were consequently much thicker and able better to hold the floor. Many of these showed bright colours in modern dyes that have mellowed little with time.

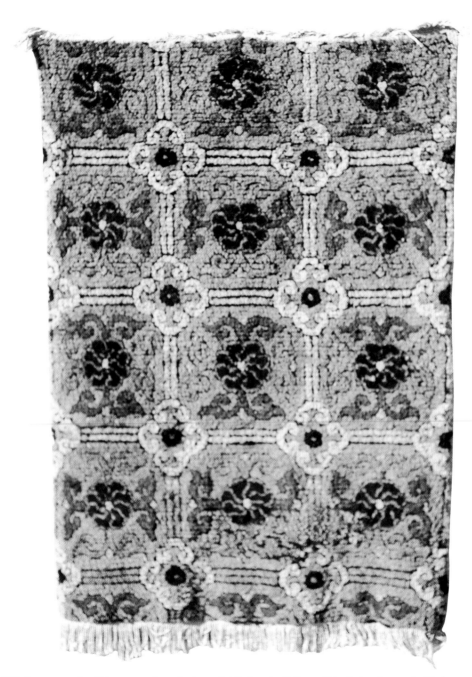

*Figure 155. Fragment of a Chinese rug from the Imperial Palace in Beijing. This design has probably been woven since the seventeenth century if not before. Despite extremely coarse knotting, these rugs achieve a curvilinear design with the use of half knots and unusual knots that may extend from one shed to the next.*

*Figure 156 (opposite). Xinjiang rug from the Khotan Oasis with a repeating floral design and a classic border. The colours are classic, and this is one of the most common Khotan designs. Approx. 40 x 38ins. (102 x 97cm).*

## IMPERIAL CHINESE RUGS

A small groups of rugs associated with the Imperial court in Beijing has survived. These are extremely well drawn, although often of even coarser weave than the commercial rugs, with densities as low as 10 asymmetrical knots per square inch. A curvilinear effect is achieved by using various kinds of half knots and drawing the pile wool diagonally from one row of knots to the next. This is facilitated by the fact that many of these rugs are unusual in that the wefts are passed only after two rows of knots. The palette also differs from the commercial rugs in being somewhat more intense. Green, seldom seen on other Chinese rugs, may be more prominent. Several dramatic rugs, some with large dragons, survive from this group, and specimens are still in the Imperial palace in Beijing (**Figure 155**).

There has been some controversy as to whether some of these rugs date from the Ming period (1368–1644), as the drawing of the dragons is consistent with that found on various Ming textiles.

So far, however, carbon dating has not confirmed that any of these rugs are datable any earlier than the last half of the seventeenth century.

## XINJIANG

Rugs from the Xinjiang province, also described as Eastern Turkestan, are often placed in a separate category from those of the rest of China. They are woven by Uighurs, a non-Chinese ethnic minority. They speak a Turkic language, many are Moslem, and their culture shows many similarities to that of the Near East.

Rugs from this area are made in the oasis towns on the periphery of the Takla Makan Desert, most prominently Khotan, Kashgar, and Yarkand (**Figure 156**). In early rug literature these rugs were often labelled as Samarkands, and at one time may have reached the West through this part of central Asia. They are much more brightly coloured than rugs usually labelled Chinese, but are also woven with the asymmetrical knot. Early rugs from Khotan have

cotton warps but dark wool wefts, an unusual feature, while later rugs have a cotton foundation. There are silk rugs from this area, and some rugs – usually labelled as Kashgars although probably made in other places as well – have silk pile with parts of the surface woven with metal-wrapped silk thread. While many of the later silk rugs may exceed 12 feet (3.65 metres) in length, they are not always finely woven. Often they show repeating designs related to such Persian designs as the herati. Among the most typical format is one involving the use of two or three rounded medallions, usually with stylised floral forms **(Figure 157)**.

Saddle rugs of Chinese type and a few tent bags similar to those associated with Near Eastern nomads are also found. The repeating pomegranate design, usually on a blue field, is common on this type, and occasionally these are found with silk pile. Rugs with the pomegranate design are usually more finely woven that other Xinjiang types. There is also a type in lattice designs that seems clearly to have been derived from earlier Moghul rugs. While there are few single niche prayer rugs from this area, a number of saffs are known with multiple prayer niches. These were also certainly woven for mosques, and the floor of the enormous Id-Kah Mosque in Kashgar is still covered with saffs.

There appears to have been a major change in the rug industry of Xinjiang about the turn of the nineteenth century. Not only do synthetic dyes appear in virtually all the twentieth century rugs – often with mauve and a particularly intense orange-red – but the traditional motifs were abandoned in favour of stiff medallion designs with a vaguely Near Eastern appearance. Xinjiang rugs from after the Second World War cover a wide range of designs, including adaptations of Persian designs and even pictorial rugs. In Urumchi, the capital of Xinjiang, there is a small production of silk with an extremely fine weave and some use of metal-wrapped thread for the field. These resemble the modern Hereke from Turkey.

Among the interesting woven products of Xinjiang are the silk ikats, whose designs appear to have changed little in the last several hundred years. This

*Figure 157 (opposite). Xinjiang rug from Khotan in the common three medallion design. This is probably the single most common format from Khotan with three small, rounded medallions set upon a red field. Most Khotan rugs of this vintage have an unusual structure of three wool wefts between the rows of knots and a cotton warp.*

*Figure 158. Chinese rugs from the Gansu region with features of both Xinjiang and Ningxia.*

technique involves tie-dying the silk warps and then adjusting them on large looms to form the intended design. While the same technique was traditionally used throughout central Asia, particularly in Uzbekistan, ikats from Khotan, for example, show characteristically bold designs with more black than would be found on Uzbeki ikats.

Rugs were also woven in the Gansu region of China **(Figure 158)** which show features of both Ningxia and Xinjiang rugs. At times they show designs associated with Xinjiang, but using colours more consistent with classical Chinese carpets.

*Figure 159. Tibetan sleeping rug with dragons shown in a more playful manner than on Chinese rugs. The Chinese dragon is associated with the emperor and is thus seldom drawn in less than a dignified way, but the Tibetan dragon has different nuances of meaning which convey no sense of power or threat.*

*Figure 160 (opposite). Tibetan sleeping rug with a design showing Chinese influence. In rare cases in which the design does not indicate a Tibetan or Chinese origin, the structure is so different as to make identification easy.*

## TIBET

Although Tibet is an autonomous region in southwest China, Tibetan rugs differ from other Chinese rugs in structure, colours and design. Perhaps most significant is the unusual manner in which these rugs are woven, which involves looping the pile yarn around the warps on the loom and then around a gauge rod held parallel to the wefts. When a row has been finished, a knife is passed along a groove in the rod, cutting the loop pulled over the rod, thus forming the pile (see Figure 4). The technique relates to types of weaving from the ancient Near East, particularly Coptic Egypt. There are archaeological finds of such fabrics, but the technique has survived only in Tibet, where it is a quick method of weaving

yielding relatively coarse pile with curvilinear designs. A rug in the most common size, slightly less than 3 x 6 feet (0.9 x 1.82 metres), can thus be woven in about seven days.

The curvilinear design is accomplished by the use of half knots and other knots stretched over three warps. There has been speculation that the technique is an ancient one in Tibet (an almost identical technique was used in Coptic Egypt) but there are no clearly datable Tibetan pieces likely to be more than several centuries old. While many of the earlier rugs were used as sleeping rugs (**Figures 159 and 160**), many are shaped like the Chinese saddle rugs, and there is a type resembling the open wings of a butterfly that seems uniquely Tibetan (**Figure 161**).

There are also small rugs used as bag faces, and even some rugs suggestive of a Turkmen ensi for use as door covers.

The colours are much livelier than on Chinese rugs, with more use of red and a brighter assortment of yellows and oranges. Designs are also distinctive. Dragons appear frequently, but in a more animated manner than on Chinese rugs. The snow lion, an adaptation of the fo-lion found on Chinese rugs, is also more fanciful. Floral forms are not so austere, and the traditional Tibetan rug often has about it a charming *naïveté*. Some designs seemed based upon Chinese brocades, and there are examples which use a Chinese colour scheme based around several shades of blue and ivory.

Rugs from Tibet were virtually unknown in the West until the abortive Tibetan rebellion against the Chinese in 1959, after which many Tibetans left the country as refugees. Not only did they bring with them their portable possessions of value, including many rugs, but they also began to weave rugs in Nepal. Since the early 1960s, the rug weaving industry has developed into a substantial export business. Now Tibetan-type rugs appear both from Tibet and from the refugee community in several Nepalese centres, most prominently Kathmandu. These rugs show an almost total abandonment of traditional designs, and some even show abstract designs associated with the last half of the twentieth century. They are usually made of a good grade of wool, either on cotton or wool foundations, and the colours on modern pieces generally favour muted earth tones. While earlier Tibetan rugs were nearly all of small size, the modern rug shows a full range of room-sized rugs.

## JAPAN

While Japan has never been an exporter of handmade pile carpets, there is some reason to believe that at times rugs were made in local designs. **Figure 162** is an example that has been attributed to Japan, along with several other types with an East Asian, but not Chinese, appearance. Some of these have a cotton pile, which is most unusual for a hand-knotted rug, although small areas, usually of white cotton, may also appear on rugs from Turkey and Iran.

*Figure 161 (opposite). Tibet saddle rug with bats in a shape found on rugs from other parts of China. These colours are brighter and combined in ways different from the typical Ningxia rug, but the draughtsmanship here gives the rug a charm of its own.*

*Figure 162. Little is known about early rug weaving in Japan, but occasionally there are rugs for which reasons for a Japanese origin are convincing. Approx. 73½ x 36½ins. (187 x 93cm).*

160

# CHAPTER 8

# RUGS FROM INDIA AND PAKISTAN

The early history of rugs from the Indian subcontinent includes those from Pakistan, as India was not divided into two separate countries – India and Pakistan – until 1947. It is thus reasonable to describe rugs made before that time as Indian, although since partition differences have arisen that often allow products of the two countries to be distinguished. New rugs from Pakistan will be considered below, pp.164, 177, 178.

## INDIA

Rugs have been woven in the Indian subcontinent at least since the thirteenth century, when they are described in written sources. During the Moghul period, beginning in 1526, the emperors controlled great wealth, and spent lavishly on art and architecture. Carpets were part of the décor of the court, and they appear in many miniature paintings, some of which depict carpets similar to surviving examples. Moghul miniature painting was highly influenced by the art of Persia, and Persian painters were employed by the Moghul court from the early sixteenth century. Consequently, there is a certain amount of controversy as to how much of the carpet art was developed locally and how much the result of Persian influence.

There is a large group of surviving red field rugs with blue or blue-green borders that is labelled by some

carpet scholars as having been woven in Persia, while others believe them to be Moghul work. The largest repository of the type is either traceable to the Maharaja of Jaipur's collection, while others of these surviving rugs are to be found in museums in Portugal and the Netherlands; some major examples survive in England. Since these three maritime powers of the sixteenth and seventeenth centuries all traded extensively with India, there is some reason to believe that most of these carpets were probably woven in India. Clearly they constitute one of the most successful commercial enterprises in the history of the hand-knotted carpet, and they still appear frequently at auction.

Other types of surviving Moghul rugs from the sixteenth and seventeenth centuries can be seen in western museums and private collections. Many are characterised by a vivid red field, produced with the insect dye lac, which was a major commercial item from India before the advent of commercial dyes.

By the eighteenth century the rug trade had diminished, and when it revived in the nineteenth century with the reawakened western enthusiasm for oriental rugs, the products of India were mostly derivative and based upon Persian models. Many were woven in room sizes and even extra-large sizes, and survivors from this period are still sought for particular decorative purposes, although they often

*Figure 163 (opposite). Indian rug of the nineteenth century with a design that is based on Persian rugs in its component parts, although one could not find a Persian rug with this colour scheme.*

*Detail of Figure 163.*

*Figure 164. Indian rug of the nineteenth century. Like the previous illustration, this design also shows a variety of Persian elements. Sometimes the difference in the colours and the wool allows a specific identification to be made.*

seem uninspired compared to the Persian rugs of the period **(Figures 163 and 164)**.

These later Indian rugs are asymmetrically knotted on a cotton foundation, in some cases with soft wool that is not durable. Many of the places where rugs were woven are to be found in the north-west of the subcontinent, although there was some weaving as far south as Hyderabad.

Kashmir has long been a source of particularly finely woven rugs, indeed some are difficult to distinguish from Persian city rugs. Currently the rugs of Kashmir are almost exclusively jufti knotted, with the knot encircling four warps rather than two. This technique is a labour-saving device and results in a rug that has a less dense pile, although the difference may not be immediately detectable on the back of the rug **(Figure 165)**. Often these rugs are woven in what is described as 'Kashmir wool', suggesting that the pile material is of a particularly high quality. Usually the wool, which comes from sheep rather than the Kashmir goat, is imported from abroad or from some other part of India. However, it is so soft as to be inappropriate for carpets intended to be used on the floor.

*Figure 165. Indian rug from Kashmir with a Persian design. Here many figures are highlighted in ivory silk, but a careful inspection reveals that the rug is jufti knotted.*

Silk rugs are also woven in Kashmir (**Figure 166**). These are available in two weaves, often described as the 'single knot' or the 'double knot'. The latter refers to use of the jufti, which produces a rug of lower quality.

Amritsar is another major Indian location producing rugs, but these are of a lower knot count than the typical Kashmir product, and the fabric tends to be loose because most of the rugs do not use double warps.

Rugs from Agra include a variety of grades, with almost all the rugs based around the classic Persian medallion rug. This is also the case with the major production centre in Agra with its large output of rugs, usually from cottage industries rather than large workshops. Little of this Indian production relates to Indian culture, but is mostly borrowed from Iran and produced under contract to foreign firms.

## PAKISTAN

While much of the rug business is based around Karachi, most of the actual weaving is done farther to the north around Lahore. This city was an important weaving centre during the Moghul period, and rug production has probably never entirely ceased in the meantime. After the Second World War and the partition of India, by the 1960s Lahore had rebounded strongly with the production of the Pakistani Bokhara, mostly based on designs of the Tekke Turkmen, although the wool was particularly soft and the colours muted.

In the following years, the Pakistani industry seemed to be searching for other types of rug to produce. In the 1970s a double-warped type in Persian designs appeared on the market, and in the late 1990s there was an output of naturally dyed rugs in designs from a variety of sources, some of them using Caucasian designs with excellent natural colours.

As in India, many of the rugs from Pakistan are now produced under contract to foreign firms that specify the designs, colours, and types of weave. Under these circumstances, this is probably a satisfactory arrangement, as it at least assures a textile that will be saleable in the West.

*Figure 166 (opposite). Kashmir pictorial rug with large areas of ivory silk, woven with the jufti knot. Kashmir rugs may be all of silk or show patches of silk. The floral rugs often show outlining of the design in ivory silk.*

*Detail of Figure 166.*

# CHAPTER 9

# RUGS FROM PERIPHERAL AREAS

One needs only to look in a store selling oriental rugs to find that there are examples not only from Asia, but also from Africa and Europe. The production of rugs involves both tradition and economics, and it is no accident that in many pre-industrial countries where sheep have been raised one also finds the manufacture of carpets.

## AFRICA

While there is archaeological evidence for the use of knotted pile in ancient Egypt, the first pile fabrics in Africa clearly intended for use as carpets date from the first half of the first millennium A.D., again from Egypt. There appear to have been several production centres. A number of examples survive in a slit-loop technique almost identical to that used in recent Tibetan rugs, and these show a wide range of designs from the pictorial to floral motifs associated with Mediterranean art of the time – a decorative style that could be described as Roman. In addition to charming pile rugs, many flatweaves from this period survive.

Islam spread rapidly across North Africa in the seventh century, and even if rug weaving had not existed earlier in Tunisia, Algeria, and Morocco, it would probably have become part of the culture at that time. Little was known about the development of this art until recently, when village and tribal rugs begun to be studied. While the rugs of various areas usually show similarities to each other, in that they are thick and coarsely knotted, with geometric designs, there is no uniformity of structure; the symmetrical knot is most commonly found, although North African examples exist with the asymmetrical knot and several variants.

It is difficult to date the production of pile rugs among the villages and nomads of North Africa, as little is known about the development of designs, and few truly early examples appear to have survived. Almost certainly the nomads and villagers wove rugs for local consumption for centuries, but large-scale production was probably not organised until the nineteenth century, when the French encouraged weaving rugs for export around Kairouan in Tunisia, Tlemcen in Algeria, and Rabat and other cities in Morocco. Many of the nineteenth and early twentieth century rugs from these areas survive, and a number are adaptations of nineteenth century Turkish designs. The Rabat rug of the twentieth century typically shows designs associated with Turkish rugs, but the reds are often based on cochineal, and the warp yarns are often S-spun in North African fashion. Most of these rugs are coarsely woven (**Figure 167**).

During the last half of the twentieth century these city rugs became less popular and were mostly replaced as export items by rugs from the countryside, including pieces made by Berbers. They usually show relatively simple geometric designs, often on an ivory field, but at times red is prominent. Blue is used less commonly in this area, although bright synthetic orange is common on many mid-twentieth century pieces. A number of the rugs show animal figures. Some of these rugs have extremely long pile, often

*Figure 167. Early twentieth century rug from the Moroccan city of Rabat. Clearly such rugs were based on Turkish designs. The earliest Rabat rugs of this type often showed a madder red, but turn of the century production more often used a cochineal red. Later Rabat rugs woven before the First World War often showed garish synthetic dyes.*

occurring on sleeping rugs, which are sometimes used with the pile surface downward. A large variety of flatweaves are also woven, many with elaborate tassels.

Some of the newer city rugs show designs borrowed from the Persian repertoire, often with crudely rendered medallions. The pile on most North African rugs is thick and fleecy, which has helped them find a place in the western market. The type of geometric designs done in ivory and brown have become so popular that machine-made carpeting in these designs is now produced.

## EUROPE

Rugs have probably been woven for many centuries in areas where sheep are raised, and there are references in classical literature suggesting that rugs were a common item of interior furnishing in Roman and later Byzantine times. Pieces of several large pictorial pile woven fabrics survive from medieval times in the German cities of Halberstadt and Quedlinburg. They are woven in the single warp knot found on Spanish rugs, and suggest a thriving art of the carpet in the eleventh and twelfth centuries.

Spanish rugs were made with a single warp knot tied on alternate warps in succeeding rows (see Figure 5). Archaeological specimens with this knot, from other areas, survive from the early centuries of the first millennium A.D., and the technique has continued in Spain even in recent times. Early Spanish weaving appears to have been centred in the areas controlled by Moslems, with designs related to Islamic art. So many early Spanish rugs survive that one could reasonably speculate that the Spanish rug industry of the fifteenth century exceeded in size that of any other part of the Mediterranean basin.

There are often similarities in the designs of Spanish rugs of the fifteenth century and products of the Ottoman Empire. At times it is difficult to be certain just where a given design originated. After the expulsion of the Moors from Spain in 1492, however, designs became more consonant with a European aesthetic, and examples of this are found in the products of the French rug weaving industries of Savonnerie and Aubusson. Many of the later Spanish rugs were apparently based on European-style textile designs

Almost certainly hand-knotted rugs were also made in other parts of Europe for many centuries. A rya rug from Scandinavia has a date suggesting it was woven in 1495, and East Prussia and parts of the Balkans have rug-weaving traditions going back hundreds of years. It seems reasonable to expect that in areas where sheep were raised, particularly if the climate was cold, some floor covering of wool was likely to have developed.

## THE BALKANS

As much of the Balkans, including Greece, Bulgaria, Romania, Yugoslavia, and parts of Hungary were occupied by the Ottomans – in some areas for centuries – it is not surprising that the weaving of pile rugs and kilims has been practised in the past. Although there was also a large Turkish population in the region, most products of this area do not simply follow Turkish models, and there is an ongoing debate as to whether this represents a survival of a pre-Turkish pile and kilim weaving tradition.

Perhaps best known of these Balkan kilims is an appealing type, usually described under the label Sarkoy, which was made in an area around the Serbian town of Pirot (**Figure 168**). These are characterised by use of an insect red and dark blue, with a small use of ivory and very small amounts of subsidiary colours. Some show niches or a series of niches like Turkish prayer rugs or saffs, although little is known about them to determine whether they were part of the local Islamic culture.

---

*Figure 168. Sarkoy kilim from the Balkan town of Pirot in Serbia. These kilims usually show a cochineal red field in which the structural elements are of dark blue or, in later pieces, black. Highlights are in ivory, and there is little use of yellow or green. Approx. 100 x 82ins. (254 x 208cm).*

Kilims from many parts of Romania show designs more in keeping with European traditions (**Figure 169**). Even very large examples were woven in one piece and show some loose ends on the back, as one finds with many Turkish kilims. Kilims from the Moldavian region of Romania usually show large stylised floral forms with an unusual colour scheme in which black and green are both more prominent than usual.

Kilims from the Oltenian region are particularly fine, with the use of wefts that are not strictly perpendicular to the warps. This allows for a curvilinear design unusual in flatweaves.

Elsewhere in the Balkans pile rugs were woven, but this is an area which remains controversial, for it is often difficult to tell which rugs were woven in Anatolia and which in Europe. A group of rugs from the seventeenth and eighteenth centuries often carry a Transylvania label, since a number of them have been found in the churches of the region and are thought by some scholars to have been woven there. Yet they resemble in structure and design other rugs known to have been woven in western Anatolia, and this encourages some carpet scholars to consider them Turkish imports into the Balkans.

Whatever pile weaving may have occurred in the Balkans in earlier times, a carpet industry was certainly started shortly after the Second World War in Romania, and this soon gained a place in the world market. These carpets are found in a variety of sizes, with some showing Turkish designs and others adaptations of Persian designs. The colours do not closely resemble the originals, often using a dull pumpkin colour rather than a bright red.

---

*Figure 169 (opposite). Bessarabian kilim from Romania. There are nearly a dozen areas in Romania that produce a characteristic type of kilim, including some which are clearly descended from European design traditions.*

*Detail of Figure 169.*

# CHAPTER 10

# FLATWOVEN RUGS

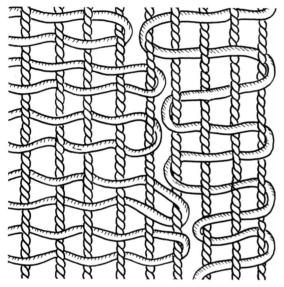

*Figure 170. Diagram of slit tapestry kilim technique showing vertical discontinuities except where there is warp sharing on warp 6. While a given area of kilim work may be accomplished much quicker than even coarsely woven pile weaving, the two fabrics are intended for such different uses that the comparison means little.*

Appreciation of flatweaves – or rugs without pile – has increased during the last three decades. While these pieces initially cost less than pile carpets and were of interest only to those with non-traditional tastes, many collectors now take them as seriously as pile weaves. Prices have correspondingly risen with demand. The term kilim is commonly used both as a general descriptive term for a flatweave, as well as for a rug produced by the specific technique known as slit tapestry. Here coloured yarns are interwoven as wefts upon undyed warps, and patches of the same colour may be staggered so that some areas are finished before others. When colour junctions occur at a vertical line, and the yarn of a given colour turns back, there may be discontinuities or slits. This may be avoided by having the yarns at colour junctions share the warp where they turn back, or there may be a complex interlock between yarns of adjacent colours. If the junctions are kept diagonal rather than vertical, the wefts' discontinuity at the junctions is not enough to seriously weaken the fabric (**Figure 170**).

## TURKISH

Kilims from Anatolia have recently become much sought after by collectors and, although usually strictly geometric, they show an amazingly varied array of designs (**Figures 171 and 172**). Many Turkish kilims are woven in two long narrow pieces, which may be joined together along a midline, when the design forms a mirror image of itself. Turkish kilims may also be woven in prayer rug designs.

*Figure 171 (opposite left). This Turkish kilim from the Karapinar region is the type woven in three pieces. The Karapinar region is also associated with a variety of pile weaves with an entirely different range of designs. The reasons why flatweave designs and those used for pile rugs could differ from the same region are varied, but in some cases it results from the two products being produced by different tribal groups living in the same area. Approx.180 x 68½ins. (457 x 174cm).*

*Figure 172 (opposite right). Turkish kilim, from the region of Aksaray, woven in two pieces. While elements of this design may also appear from other parts of Turkey, the way it is drawn here is specifically associated with Aksaray. Approx.170 x 60ins. (432 x 152cm).*

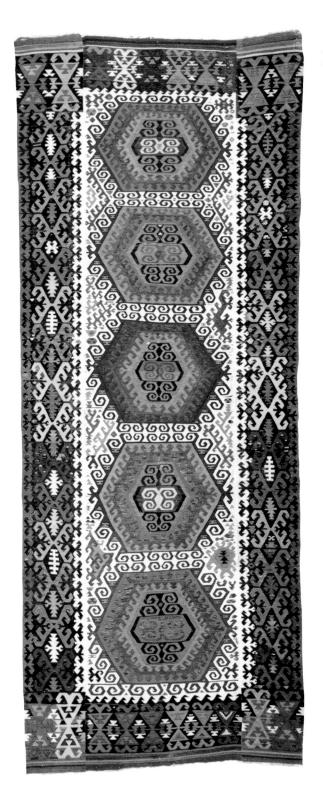

There is some controversy as to whether the traditional Turkish kilim predated the Turkic migrations into Anatolia or whether it was brought by the Turks from their homeland in central Asia. While it seems most probable that there are elements of both traditions surviving in the Turkish kilim today, it is interesting to note that little trace of designs associated with Turkish kilims survives in the parts of central Asia from which the Turks, particularly the Seljuks, set off on their migrations which brought them into Anatolia.

At the same time those groups in Turkey who have remained at least semi-nomadic into modern times are often those most closely associated with kilim weaving, and much of the output of kilims has been associated with the nomadic lifestyle. In this setting kilims are not used so much as floor coverings – which is rare – but as decorative trappings and utilitarian bags and covers. It is also interesting that the groups weaving kilims are not so likely to be producers of pile weaves, who are most often found in settled villages.

While kilim design of the last several centuries would appear on the surface to be non-representational, one may learn to recognise stylised floral forms based on carnations, tulips, and other plants.

A number of Turkish kilim types have achieved particular prominence. The Yuncu kilim, woven in the area of Balikesir, is recognised as of particular interest. It is usually characterised by an overall design – rather than by compartments in which the motifs are repeated – and a dark blue and red colour scheme in which there are often ivory highlights.

## PERSIAN

Perhaps the most finely woven near eastern kilims of the last several centuries are those of Senneh in Iran. Although they are not so fine as some pre-Columbian textiles of the Andes, and a number of extremely fine Coptic textiles from Egypt, they often convey a curvilinear design, which is rare with this technique. This involves the insertion of wefts so that there are not always the same number of threads from one area to the next, and some of the wefts are inserted at angles other than ninety degrees. Usually the kilims of a given region seem to bear no relationship to the pile weaves, but the Senneh kilim uses essentially the

same range of designs. The repeating boteh design is common, as are renditions of the herati design. Such finely woven fabrics were surely intended for decorative rather than utilitarian uses.

Most Persian kilims, however, are woven for a variety of functions. Some are used as curtains, separating parts of the nomadic tent or the small village dwelling. Many are woven as bags for food items such as bread or salt. Some function as spreads on which meals are served. The nomadic Baluchi and the Afshars produce a number of small flatweaves having to do with the serving of meals.

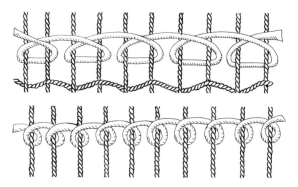

*Figure 173. Diagram of the soumak technique of weft wrapping. Row 1 shows the yarn wrapped under two and over four warps from right to left, while Row 2 shows a wrapping over two and under one warp from left to right. A single ground weft is shown. A number of small bags from the Caucasus are woven in what is described as reverse soumak, in which the back becomes the surface and the loose ends are left on the side usually used as the surface.*

## SOUMAK

The flatweave known as soumak uses a weft-wrapping technique made on a loom on which coloured wefts are wrapped around warps until a colour junction is reached, where they reverse direction or the loose ends are left at the back of the fabric. The yarn first encircles four warps and then the last two warps, causing the next loop to lie at a slight angle. This may also be accomplished in other multiples, and then the next row is usually slanted in the opposite direction. There are numerous variations, including some fabrics with extra undyed ground wefts and others without (**Figure 173**).

*Figure 174. Caucasian rug in soumak technique with a design originally based upon dragon figures. These pieces were formerly known under the name sileh, but the recent literature has suggested that verneh is a more correct term.*

Soumak weaving occurs in most places where rugs are woven, except for the Far East. Soumaks from the Caucasus are particularly sought by collectors **(Figure 174)**, as are soumak tribal pieces – usually bag faces – from parts of Iran and Turkey. Soumak is seldom finely rendered enough to produce curvilinear designs, although the fabric may be sturdy enough to serve as floor covering.

*Figure 175. Turkmen bag in which the design is rendered in a weft float technique.*

required for the design. This technique is often used for a band of design in the kilim ends of Baluchi rugs and is most frequently found in Iran.

Warp float and warp substitution – which differ slightly – are often used in the weaving of long strips, such as Turkmen tent bands. Here the warps are dyed, often in two colours, but sometimes more. As in weft substitution, a given colour appears on the surface when it is required for the design. Many of these bands approach 50 feet (15.24 metres) in length. Some are woven on primitive looms, while others are woven on looms in which the sheds are opened by pedals.

## EMBROIDERY

Fabrics described as embroidered are decorated on a foundation cloth using a needle and various coloured threads with which the design is slowly constructed. Embroideries have a wide distribution, although they have not proved such a popular commercial item as pile carpets. The embroideries of most interest to rug collectors in general include several types from the Caucasus, most prominently those woven in Azerbaijan, often in designs familiar from an earlier generation of carpets, and those produced by Armenian women. From the northern Caucasus come the Kaitag embroideries of Daghestan.

The Turkmen have also produced elaborately embroidered ceremonial garments for women, and decorated cuffs and collars for the men. Uzbekis also produce the embroidered suzanis that are becoming popular with collectors. Villages in parts of Iran and Turkey are also known for embroidered fabrics, while the Chinese have long been masters of this art, producing large and labour intensive embroideries in silk.

## BROCADES

Brocading involves the use of extra weft yarns to decorate a fabric. There are number of techniques, but they impose restrictions on the design. While a brocade design can be copied in pile or soumak, a design in either of these techniques cannot necessarily be copied in brocade. Anatolia is probably the richest source of a variety of brocades, although there are less common brocades in Iran and among the Turkmen. **(Figure 175)**. As with soumak and slit-tapestry, brocaded fabrics may function as covers or for various types of bag faces, and some are heavy enough for floor use.

## WEFT AND WARP SUBSTITUTION FABRICS

Another type of fabric woven in most areas where pile rugs are made involves the use of coloured wefts or warps that are brought to the surface at appropriate intervals to form the desired design. Weft substitution (sometimes called weft float) is the most common, usually in two colours but occasionally more. Wefts of various colours traverse the width of the rug and are brought to the surface when a particular colour is

CHAPTER 11

# MODERN RUGS

One might assume that contemporary rugs are not particularly difficult to identify, but there are many complications. Some new rugs have a label sewn on the back indicating where they were woven, but most do not. For most recent products neither structure nor design are reliable indicators, for traditional rug designs are, for better or worse, perceived as common property. A traditional Persian design can appear in adaptations from China, India, Pakistan, and even Egypt, which has recently begun producing rugs.

The most important requirement for rug manufacturing is a ready supply of inexpensive labour. Wool can and often is imported from another country, and designs can be adapted from many sources, including existing rugs or pictures. Copies of Caucasian designs may be found from Pakistan, and even the gabbeh rugs, formerly made by village and tribal people in Iran, have now become a big business in which professional designers are able to create just the right 'primitive' look.

Turkmen rugs were among the first since the Second World War to be copied in other places, and the so-called 'Pakistani Bokhara' was mostly adapted from designs of the Tekke. There is little likelihood of mistaking one type for the other, however, as the Tekke is woven on a wool foundation of a rather firm wool that wears well in carpets. The Pakistani version is woven on a cotton foundation, and the wool pile is often from merino wool imported from New Zealand or other wool exporting countries. It is especially soft and lacks durability, although the rugs may be as finely knotted as the originals.

Some adaptations of Persian city rugs are not easy to tell from the original, as the foundation in both cases is ordinarily cotton, and the wool may be a reasonably good match for the original. Several decades ago the colours on Persian adaptations from India and Pakistan were often subtly wrong enough so that one could distinguish the copy from the original, but recently the manufacturers – who often work under contract to large western concerns – have managed convincing colour matches so that one may look at an adaptation of a Persian Kerman, for example, and not be certain whether it is contemporary Iranian, Pakistani, Indian, or Chinese.

One might wonder whether this makes any difference, and here one should consider the various prejudices of the market. Ordinarily rugs from Iran have sold for more money than pieces with the same designs from other places. They are not necessarily better made, but in some poorly defined way they are seen as the originals, while those from other places are seen as copies or reproductions. Thus the price one pays for a rug may well relate directly to its country of origin. If one were to sell a given rug in thirty years, the price obtained for it might still relate to perceptions about its place of origin. Of course this aspect of the market is difficult to predict, and the passage of time may mean that other factors than place of origin predominate.

The purpose for which the rug is intended is also a factor. The person whose main interest is purchasing an attractive floor covering may have no concern at all about where the design originated and who wove it. For the collector, however, focusing on older rugs, how the rug is to be displayed is extremely important.

## HOW SUCCESSFUL ARE NEW RUGS?

Apart from the concept of authenticity, which may or may not be important to the individual rug buyer, rugs may also be extremely decorative and successful in their own terms.

In previous decades, communication between countries making rugs and those buying them was poor, and western markets were provided with goods made by people without a clear concept of what would be successful in those markets. Now styles are subject to change just as fashions evolve in other arts. At times rugs in earth tones are in style, and at other

*Figure 176. Modern Pakistani rug in natural dyes based upon seventeenth century Persian designs. Some of these rugs so expertly approximate Persian designs that in many cases there is no clear way to distinguish the Persian rug from a copy.*

*Figure 177 (opposite). Modern Indian rug in natural dyes with a design adapted from seventeenth century Moghul court designs.*

times deep maroon and dark blues are the top selling types. Shortly after the Second World War, the Kerman rug from Iran was woven in pastel colours, with extra-thick pile and open fields often of ivory. Two decades later it had returned more to its early twentieth century tradition of elaborate designs in stronger colours and shorter pile.

Today the needs of the market are communicated with great immediacy and clarity to the manufacturers, and often the importers order designs based upon their conception of what the market is at the moment or will likely be in the next few years. The degree of success importers enjoy depends upon their skill in reading the wishes of their customers, and many in the business look upon this as a great advance over the times when they were left with the task of selling what producers wanted to make. Thus

contemporary rugs exported from Tibet, for example, are still woven in the same unusual manner as before, but now they appear almost exclusively in designer patterns, at times based upon western modern art. However, the structure of a rug is no longer a reliable guide as to where it was woven, and increasingly the new rugs are not identifiable by the criteria noted in preceding chapters for the traditional weaving areas.

## REVIVAL OF NATURAL DYES

One advantage of the new production of rugs is the revival of natural dyes, where the buyer is increasingly able to find rugs woven using traditional colours. A movement began to gather momentum in the 1970s, when several Americans in Kathmandu began experimenting with natural dyes, and a German chemist working with some weavers from western

Turkey founded the DOBAG project. Soon other pilot projects investigating the use of natural dyes were operating in Afghanistan and Pakistan.

The movement has grown rapidly, and the results are impressive. By the early 1990s a large output of naturally-dyed rugs began to flow from the Shiraz region of Iran. Often these were woven in the rather thick, coarsely knotted gabbeh style, but the colours were splendid, and the rugs found ready markets. Rugs based on the designs of Persian cities and from Moghul India are now appearing with natural dyes **(Figures 176, 177, and 178).**

*Figure 178. Modern Indian rug based upon earlier designs with the colours mellowed by what is described as a tea wash, which superficially gives an appearance of age. When the rug receives a wash that alters the appearance of every colour, and often even the fringe, then there appears to be no good reason for there to be natural dyes.*

The reds in these natural-dyeing projects are almost all based around madder. Cochineal has become particularly expensive, and the types of rug to which natural dyes make the most important contribution are not those few types that traditionally use insect dyes. Whether the natural dyers use natural indigo or synthetic is probably of little importance, but making a green with a combination of indigo and a yellow dyes gives a far richer result, often with a variegated effect in which there are highlights of both colours distributed in an appealing way. Purple shades from a combination of red and blue dyes are also preferable to the synthetic purples.

There is some question as to whether all the rugs said to be naturally dyed actually meet the standard. Since the rugs generally seem well coloured, one seldom thinks to challenge the dyes on a given rug. Yet the competing dealers who commission many of these rugs often criticise the colours of their competitors' rugs as not really being from natural sources. It is not inconceivable that some of the claims may be exaggerated.

## OLD VERSUS NEW

While there are many who bemoan the loss of tradition in the oriental rug business, the new rug sector seems surprisingly healthy, and there are probably more new rugs of high quality available now than at any time since the late nineteenth century. The question arises as to whether these rugs should be seen as successful reproductions, or whether they are works of art in their own right. To many potential buyers this concept makes no difference at all. They purchase rugs with which to cover the floor, and they approach this in the same way they would the purchase of a dining room set or a dressing table for the bedroom. While these pieces of furniture may be based upon earlier styles from the seventeenth century French court or eighteenth century early American furniture, the buyer knows he is acquiring a reproduction and is perfectly satisfied with that concept.

Is a print of a Rembrandt, or even a careful copy in oils on canvas, an acceptable substitute? Is there a difference? The answer depends on many factors, including what the buyer is willing to pay.

For those who see a fine oriental rug as a work of art, however, the difference is crucial, and the issue becomes not so much the accuracy with which a given design is rendered, but upon finer aesthetic points involving the circumstances under which the rug was woven. While a design can be copied, the sensibilities of the work's creator involve subtleties and nuances that allow a committed carpet connoisseur to single out one rug in a given design as a deeply felt artistic masterpiece while rejecting another version as a work of secondary importance. When asked to explain their preferences, few rug enthusiasts seem as skilful with words as they are in their appreciation, but several concepts emerge.

Perhaps most important is the idea that the seventeenth century nomad in a remote part of Turkey had such a different set of life experiences that her concepts of nature, god, morality, and beauty are likely to differ substantially from our own. Almost always the weaver will have been a woman, whose role in life several centuries ago would have been far different from the role of a contemporary woman, and it is certain she would be illiterate and have not the slightest formal training in aesthetics. Within this milieu, which she may experience as both frightening and emotionally rewarding, she creates something of beauty for the use of her family, perhaps to be passed on to future generations. Since it will occupy hundreds of hours work over a period of months, and since it

will be produced within the home in which she gives care to her children, it seems at least plausible that she will put something powerfully personal into this rug.

This 'something' may or may not be recognisable as to meaning, although many early peasant and nomad rugs have a variety of figures that seem to be scattered at random within the overall design. What the true believer perceives, however, is something that communicates across the great cultural gap between us and the weavers. The best of these rugs possess a quality not impossible to find in a recent rug – although it is probably more prevalent from an earlier time – that elicits a deeply satisfying feeling from the viewer. Whether one calls it folk art, decorative art, or the high art of the particular culture from which it arises, it still conveys a feeling, a sense of pleasure, a reward to the senses.

The other side of the spectrum is the factory-produced rug that dominates the market today. Here we have weavers who may be perfectly competent, but who either work in a large workshop or who may work at home but with a design, wool, and loom supplied by businessmen who commission rugs on a piecework basis. The design may be from a different country or culture than that to which the weaver belongs, and it may not even be to her taste. She may share the loom with another weaver of a slightly different background, and they may spend the day gossiping as they tie knot after knot. Not surprisingly, this is what is known in the West as a 'job', and it often involves little of the weavers' inner selves. The weavers here are assembly line workers who follow directions and are not expected to put anything of themselves into their work.

So when we consider the well dyed, competently designed, workshop made new rugs that are often extremely attractive pieces of home furnishings, we return to the question of what rug buyers want and believe they are purchasing. If they want home furnishings, there are excellent examples of new rugs to be purchased. It is quite another matter if the buyers are looking for art. Distinguishing the difference is not a simple matter and not to be accomplished by reading a basic guidebook, but the author hopes this volume will provide a start.

CHAPTER 12

# WHERE TO SEE ORIENTAL RUGS

Where best to see oriental rugs depends upon which kinds of rugs one finds of interest. Rugs significant to the history of the art are almost all in museum collections, although some of the great court carpets are so large that they take up the space of many paintings and are thus difficult to display. Consequently even the most important museums often do not have space to exhibit their entire rug collections, and some museums alternate their exhibits so that one may not always find a given rug on display even if it is known to be in the possession of a particular museum. It is always wise to contact a museum before visiting to check that it is open and that particular rugs are on display at the time.

The best collections of historically significant carpets are in the following museums:

The **Victoria and Albert Museum, London**, has the best of its carpet collection on permanent display, and this includes the largest of the two Ardabil carpets with an inscribed date. It also has the important so-called Chelsea carpet, a major collection of early Spanish rugs, and an assortment of other major historical pieces.

There are several significant carpets in **Oxford's Ashmolean Museum**. While there are some interesting carpets at **Hampton Court Palace** and in various English stately homes, there are no other substantial permanent museum collections in the United Kingdom.

The **Metropolitan Museum of Art, New York**, has a splendid collection which includes one of the so-called Emperor's carpets (the other is in Vienna), some excellent Ottoman court pieces, and major Moghul and Persian Safavid pieces. The **Philadelphia Museum of Art** shows some major Safavid examples on permanent display, as well as some excellent early Turkish carpets. The **Textile Museum in Washington, D.C.**, has an excellent collection of important carpets, but exhibition space is

so limited that at any given time there may be nothing significant for the rug collector on display. The same warning applies to the **DeYoung Museum, San Francisco**, which possesses over a thousand carpets and kilims, including probably the world's best public collection of Turkmen rugs, but at any given time only a handful of examples will be on display.

In continental Europe the **Austrian Museum of Applied Art, Vienna**, certainly has the best collection, including major Safavid and Moghul pieces, and there are also major examples to be seen in the **State Museum of Berlin**, which includes a number of pieces of great historical significance on permanent display. Otherwise rugs are spread among a number of German city museums, including the **Museum for Applied Art, Frankfurt**, and the **Museum for Art and Industry, Hamburg**. Both have small but significant collections.

In France the **Musée des Tissus, Lyon**, has a permanent display of some of the most important surviving rugs, including excellent Safavid material. Some rugs, formerly part of the collection of the Musée des Arts Décoratifs, are now exhibited in the **Musée du Louvre, Paris**.

Some of the many classic carpets now in museums elsewhere came to light in Italy during the late nineteenth century, and there are still some excellent pieces to be found in the **Bardini Museum, Florence**, and the **Pitti Palace, Florence**. The **Poldi Pezzoli Museum, Milan**, displays a small collection, including one of the most important dated Safavid rugs.

A number of Spanish museums have important collections, particularly of Spanish rugs. In Portugal the **Gulbenkian Museum, Lisbon**, displays a number of significant classical carpets.

For a thorough understanding of Turkish rugs there is no substitute for a visit to **Istanbul**, where parts of an immense collection of early Turkish rugs are always on display at the **Museum of Turkish and Islamic**

**Art**. Carpets in the **Vakiflar Museum** are also of major importance. Examples in both places have been gathered together mostly from the mosques of Turkey.

The two museums in which carpets are displayed in **Ashghabat**, the capital of Turkmenistan, are new, and some of the rugs are relatively recent, but this remains a place where one may become familiar with the range of Turkmen rugs. There is also a smaller collection in **Merv**, while Central Asian rugs are also well represented in two museums in **Tashkent** and one in **Samarkand**.

In the **Islamic Art Museum, Cairo**, are two of the important Salting group of carpets, now understood to be Safavid work, as well as a number of Turkish prayer rugs. The **Coptic Museum, Cairo**, has the world's largest collection of pile carpets from first millennium A.D. Egypt.

There is a carpet Museum in **Baku, Azerbaijan**, with a large collection of early Caucasian carpets, while a museum in **Erivan** is reputed to have over one thousand early Caucasian carpets, though some travellers have complained that it is difficult to find it open.

The **Carpet Museum, Tehran**, occupies a large new building displaying several important classical carpets and an excellent collection of Persian carpets, mostly city rugs, from the nineteenth century.

Collectors interested in seeing more recent rugs than those to be found in museum collections are referred to any conveniently located commercial establishment. The bazaars in Istanbul and Tehran contain vast numbers of rugs, and most large cities have extensive rug emporiums. The auction rooms in New York, London, and Wiesbaden, Germany, provide an excellent opportunity to view rugs of the sort currently coming on to the collector's market.

Altogether there is ample opportunity throughout the world for those interested in rugs to see and experience everything from the finest to the most recent commercial rugs.

# GLOSSARY

**abrash** – variation in single colour throughout a rug (Figure 22)
**asmalyk** – decorative five-sided trapping used in wedding ceremony
**asymmetrical knot** – see knot

**boteh** – pear-shaped motif, appearing in curvilinear and rectilinear form (Figure 15)
**brocading** – use of extra weft yarns to decorate a fabric
**broken border** – interrupted border allowing the field to encroach into the border

**chuval** – large tent bag
**curvilinear design** – with flowing lines (Figure 12)
**cut loop technique** – (Figure 4)

**double-warped** – tightly pulled wefts create warps on two levels

**ensi** – woven door covering for a yurt
**ertmen gul** – see gul

**field** – area of rug between the border and the central design
**flatweave** – rug without pile

**gabbeh** – thick, coarse symmetrically-knotted rug with simple geometric designs
**geometric design** –with angular lines (Figure 13)
**Gördes knot** – see knot
**guard stripe** – narrower, minor border
**gul** – characteristic tribal motif; the ertmen gul is a stepped or halved gul form; the tauk noshka gul is a quartered gul form; the kepse gul is a form of stylised palmette

**ikat** – resist dyeing technique

**jufti knot** – see knot

**kepse gul** – see gul
**kilim** – general term for a flatweave rug; rug produced in the slit tapestry technique
**knot** – segment of pile yarn tied round warp threads. Figure 2 shows the symmetrical Turkish or Gördes knot; Figure 3 the asymmetrical Persian or Senneh knot; the asymmetrical jufti knot is tied around four warps, a labour-saving device giving a less dense pile
**kufesque border** – border said to be based on Kufic lettering

**loom** – structure on which the warp is positioned

**medallion** – single large figure, usually symmetrical, in centre of rug (Figure 14)
**mihrab** – arched niche in a prayer rug, pointing towards Mecca (Figure 19)
*mille fleurs* **design** – literally thousand flowers design; pattern of small scattered flowers

**ok-bash** – bag for tent pegs or spindles

**Persian knot** – see knot
**pile** – segments of knotted yarn forming the design of a rug
**pileless weave** – see flatweave
**prayer rug** – rug with asymmetric design with a niche (mihrab) at one end (Figure 19)

**runner** – long rug

**S-spun yarn** – direction in which the yarn is spun (Figure 11)
**saff** – large prayer rug with multiple mihrabs, used in mosques (Figure 20)
**selvage** – side edging or finish of a rug

**Senneh knot** – see knot
**shoot** – row of weft yarn between each row of knots
**slit tapestry** – pileless technique in which areas of discontinuous coloured weft are separated by slits (Figure 170)
**soumak** – type of flatweave employing extra weft wrapping (Figure 174)
**suzani** – emboidered hanging, ususally featuring flowers
**symmetrical knot** – see knot

**tauk noshka gul** – see gul
**tea wash** – wash giving superficial appearance of age to a rug (Figure 178)
**tent band** – long, narrow functional or decorative weaving found in a yurt
**torba** – type of tent bag
**Turkish knot** – see knot

**warp** – yarn wound round a loom, to be crossed by the weft
**warp float** – see warp substitution
**warp substitution** – warps of two or more colours run the length of, for example, a tent band and are brought to the top when appropriate for the design
**weft** – yarn crossing the warp
**weft float** – see weft substitution
**weft substitution** – wefts of various colours run the width of the rug and are brought to the top when appropriate for the design (Figure 175)

**yastik** – pillow cover
**yatak** – square rug for sleeping, usually from Konya area
**yurt** – circular felt tent

**Z-spun yarn** – direction in which the yarn is spun (Figure 11)

# SELECTED BIBLIOGRAPHY

Chris Alexander, *A Foreshadowing of 21st Century Art*, Oxford University Press, New York, 1993.

Belkis Balpinar and Udo Hirsch, *Carpets of the Vakiflar Museum, Istanbul*, Uta Hülsey, Wesel, 1988.

Ferenc Batari, *Ottoman Turkish Carpets*, Applied Arts Museum, Budapest, 1994.

May H. Beattie, *The Thyssen-Bornemisza Collection of Oriental Rugs*, Castagnola, 1972.

May H. Beattie, *Carpets of Central Persia*, World of Islam Festival Publishing Co., Sheffield, 1976.

W. Brüggemann and H. Böhmer, *Rugs of the Peasants and Nomads of Anatolia*, Munich, 1983.

P. Davies, *The Tribal Eye: Antique Kilims of Anatolia*, New York, 1993.

Maurice Dimand and Jean Mailey, *Oriental Rugs in the Metropolitan Museum of Art,* Metropolitan Museum of Art, New York, 1973.

Dennis Dodds and Murray Eiland, Jr., *Oriental Rugs from Atlantic Collections*, 8th ICOC, Philadelphia, 1996.

Murray L. Eiland, Jr., *Chinese and Exotic Rugs*, New York Graphic Society, Boston, 1979,

M.L. Eiland, Jr., and M.L. Eiland, III, *Oriental Rugs, a Complete Guide*, Calmann & King, London, 1998.

Kurt Erdmann (ed. Hanna Erdmann), *Seven Hundred Years of Oriental Rugs,* University of California Press, Berkeley, 1970.

Charles Grant Ellis, *Early Caucasian Rugs*, The Textile Museum, Washington, D.C., 1975.

Charles Grant Ellis, *Oriental Carpets in the Philadelphia Museum of Art*, Philadelphia Museum of Art, Philadelphia, 1988.

Michael Franses and Rupert Waterhouse (eds.), *Classical Chinese Carpets I*, Textile and Art Publications, London, 1999.

E. Gans Ruedin, *Indian Carpets*, Rizzoli, New York, 1984.

Heinrich Kirchheim, et al., *Orient Stars*, E. Heinrish Kirchheim and HALI Publications, Stuttgart and London, 1993.

Ernst Kühnel and Louisa Bellinger, *Catalogue of Spanish Rugs: 12th Century to nineteenth Century*, The Textile Museum, Washington, 1953.

Ernst Kühnel and Louisa Bellinger, *Cairene Rugs and Others Technically Related: 15th–17th Century*, National Publishing Co., Washington, 1957.

H.A. Lorentz, *A View of Chinese Rugs*, Routledge & Kegan Paul, London, 1973.

Joseph V. McMullan, *Islamic Carpets*, New York, 1965.

Marla Mallett, *Woven Structures: a Guide to Oriental Rug and Textile Analysis*, Atlanta, 1998.

Lucy der Manuelian and Murray Eiland, Jr., *Weavers, Merchants, and Kings: the Inscribed Rugs of Armenia*, Kimbell Art Museum, Fort Worth, 1984.

Nazan Ölçer et al., *Turkish Carpets from the 13th–18th Centuries*, Istanbul, 1996.

Arthur Upham Pope, *A Survey of Persian Art*, 6 vols., Oxford University Press, London, 1938-9.

Friedrich Sarre and Hermann Trenkwald, *Old Oriental Carpets*, 2 vols, Leipzig, 1926–29.

Ulrich Schürmann, *Caucasian Rugs*, Braunschweig, 1979.

Serare Yetkin, *Early Caucasian Carpets in Turkey*, Oguz Press, London, 1978.

Friedrich Spuhler, *Oriental Carpets in the Museum of Islamic Art, Berlin*, Faber & Faber, London, 1987.

Daniel Walker, *Flowers Underfoot: Indian Carpets of the Mughal Era*, Metropolitan Museum of Art, New York, 1998.

Richard Wright and John Wertime, *Caucasian Carpets and Covers*, HALI Publications, London, 1995.

**RUSSIA**

*Caucasus Mountains*

*Black Sea*

**GEORGIA**

Tbilisi

**ISTANBUL**

Hereke

Ladik

Kars

*Sea of Marmara*

Erzerum

**ARMENIA**

Çanakkale

Ankara

Erivan

Bergama

Kirshehir

Izmir

Demirci

**TURKEY**

Malatya

Tabriz

Konya

Diyarbekir

Milas

Karapinar

Rhodes

**SYRIA**

*Kurds*

**CYPRUS**

**LEBANON**

*Mediterranean Sea*

**IRAQ**

**ISRAEL**

**JORDAN**

**EGYPT**

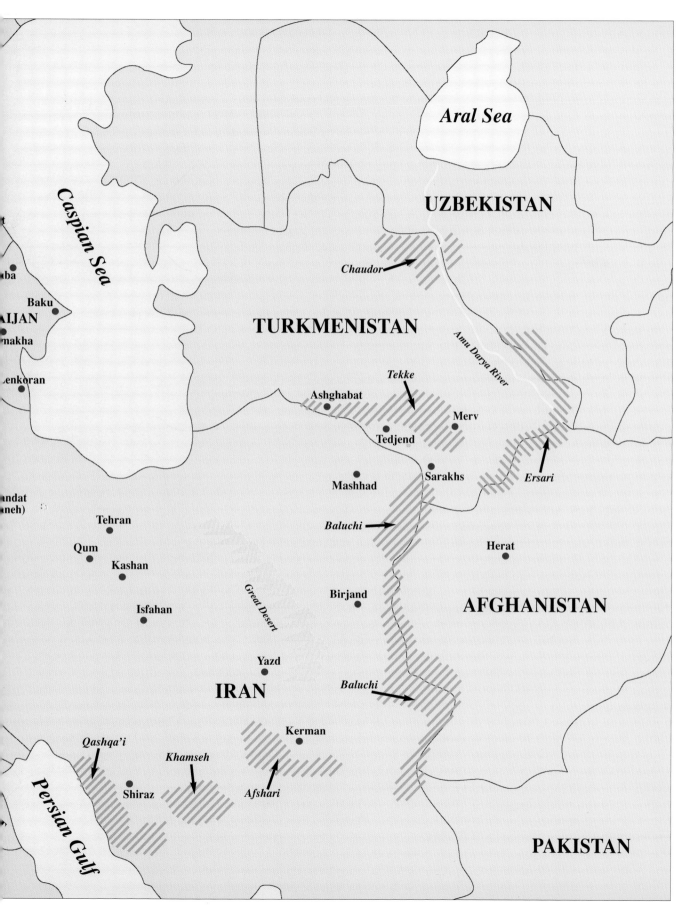

*Aral Sea*

UZBEKISTAN

*Caspian Sea*

*Chaudor*

TURKMENISTAN

*Amu Darya River*

Baku

AIJAN

makha

Lenkoran

*Tekke*

Ashghabat

Merv

Tedjend

*Ersari*

Sarakhs

Mashhad

ndat
neh)

Tehran

*Baluchi*

Qum

Kashan

Herat

Isfahan

*Great Desert*

Birjand

AFGHANISTAN

Yazd

IRAN

*Baluchi*

Kerman

*Qashqa'i*

*Khamseh*

*Persian Gulf*

Shiraz

*Afshari*

PAKISTAN

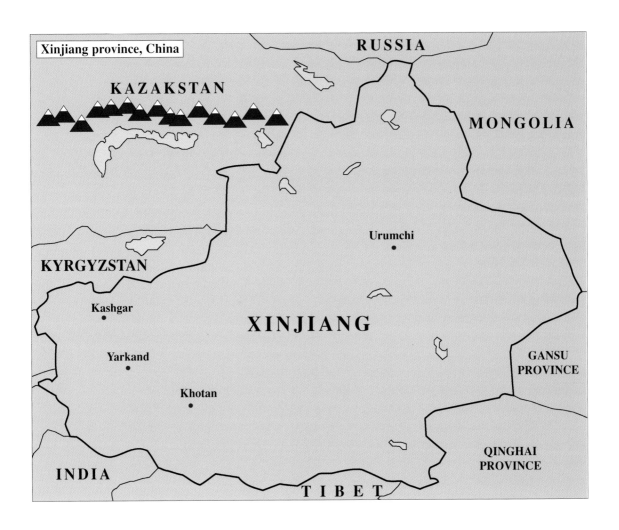

Xinjiang province, China

RUSSIA

KAZAKSTAN

MONGOLIA

KYRGYZSTAN

Urumchi

Kashgar

XINJIANG

GANSU
PROVINCE

Yarkand

Khotan

QINGHAI
PROVINCE

INDIA

TIBET

# Picture Credits

Figures 17, 21, 30, 34, 35, 36, 41, 42, 50, 52, 54, 58, 60, 63, 66, 73, 75, 79, 83, 85, 99, 100, 103, 104, 121, 123, 127, 128, 130, 134, 137, 139, 140, 141, 143, 150, 151, 156, 162, 168, 169, 171, 172 courtesy of Rippon Boswell and Co., Wiesbaden.

Figures 15, 19, 37, 44, 46, 56, 61, 100, 101, 106, 112, 116, 129, 152, 158, 175 courtesy of Taher Sabahi of *Ghereh*, International Carpet and Textile Review, Torino.

Figures 12, 14, 18, 22, 23, 27, 28, 31, 33, 38, 39, 40, 44, 48, 49, 51, 53, 65, 93, 112, 163, 164 courtesy of Roger and Conroy Cavanna of Carpets of the Inner Circle, San Francisco.

Figures 78, 81, 108, 148, 149 courtesy of the Jim Dixon Collection.

Figures 176, 177, 178 courtesy of Emmett Eiland Oriental Rugs, Berkeley.

Figures 147, 154, 157 courtesy of Sandra Whitman, San Francisco.

Figures 113, 114 courtesy of Dr. D. Gilbert and Hillary Dumas, Berkeley.

Figures 2, 3, 4, 9, 11, 170, and 173 were drawn by Dania Mallette.

# INDEX

Page numbers in bold refer to illustrations

190